5 Kids, 1 Wife

SCOTT TENNANT

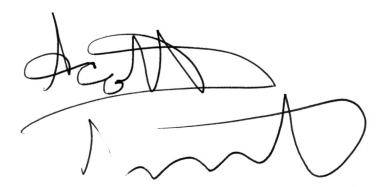

5 Kids, 1 Wife

Copyright © Scott Tennant 2023

All rights reserved. No part of this book may be reproduced, or stored in a retrieval system or transmitted in any form or by any means, electronic, mechanical, photocopying, recording or otherwise, without the prior approval of the author.

ISBN: 979-8-9888237-0-4 (paperback)
979-8-9888237-1-1 (ebook)

Published by: Blue Devil Publishing

Printed in the United States of America

Cover design: Callie Bumba
Page layout and production: Catherine Williams, Chapter One Book Production, UK

This book wouldn't exist without my wife Terry and my children Elissa, Chloe, Jared, Melanie and Jack. In some respects, neither would I.

Contents

Foreword 1

Acknowledgements 3

PARENTING

The world begins evaluating your children the moment they're born . . . 7

The necessary evil of Chuck E. Cheese 11

We already hug our kids a little tighter 14

When a child chunders 17

The art of dadness 20

The Lazy Person's Guide to Parent-Teacher Conferences 24

The end of the innocence (but not yet) 28

It's not my fault, says the youngster before me 30

The numbing realization that no parent really has any idea
   what they're doing 33

Boosting the confidence of your less-confident kids 36

Remember when kids used to have their summers free? 40

I would have been fine with a house full of daughters, but sons
   are nice, too 44

What I miss and what I don't miss about having babies in the house . . . 47

Should you have another child? Here's my advice 50

WHY did you have kids? 53

Five things I want to tell my son on this, the day of his high school
   graduation 55

I was Daddy. Now I am Dad. 59

My early approach to parenting depended heavily on Barney and
    Pooh Bear videos 62

RELATIONSHIPS & FAMILY LIFE

1986: Mr. Cool takes his girl out on the town 67

Family movie night: Popcorn and trauma 72

Mr. Please-Don't-Fix-It 75

What people in my family actually mean when they say
    certain things 78

Did I ever tell you about the time my wife dumped me? Twice? 80

These, believe it or not, are your finest days 84

The 40-Year-Old Nephew 87

Someone you love dies once, but you miss them forever 89

Marrying young ... however you define "young" nowadays 91

He was my friend 94

OTHER THINGS ON MY MIND

What your choice of board game says about you 99

Put me in, Coach (or at least give me a brownie) 102

Five songs that make dads of daughters start blubbering 106

Psychoanalysis through band instruments 110

Our new thousand-dollar dishwasher 115

One soldier's life, long forgotten 118

The story of my vasectomy you didn't ask for 120

An October roller coaster of emotions 123

I just assume you're a good person (or "The time I gave $80 to a stranger
    named Maurice") 136

Dear random number that texted me 140

The smell of pipe tobacco, four decades later 142

My mom used to give me a dollar to go and buy a loaf of Italian
    bread at Fazio's. I got to keep 25 cents. 144

"Hi guy!" Did your hometown (like mine) have its own unique catchphrase? 146

Why I never took another shop class after 8th grade 148

When I was a freshman in high school, the seniors seemed like adults to me 150

Here's why I was on the local TV news in 1977 (and never really saw it) 152

These are the non-icky details of my colonoscopy 155

My failure of the month (and why everyone telling you how great you are at something may not be the best thing) 161

I love the concept of beach vacations. It's the execution that gives me problems 165

THE GAME SHOWS

My 15 minutes (maybe 20) of TV fame were up long ago 171

It's my book and I can talk about the fact I was on two game shows any time I want 176

This is a quick story about me and Ken Burns 178

Epilogue 181

Foreword

There are some things you should know:

- Each of these 51 essays was originally a post on my blog "5 Kids, 1 Wife" (5kids1wife.com).
- There are hundreds of posts there that didn't make the cut for this book, some of which may be worth your time in case you ever want to visit.
- The main characters in these little missives are my wife Terry and my kids (in birth order) Elissa, Chloe, Jared, Melanie and Jack. I freely toss these names around as if you know who they are, so in case you don't, I hope that helps.
- The date you see near the top of each post is, as you might imagine, the date it originally appeared online. Each is written from the perspective of the time it was published.
- I am undeserving of the life I lead. I take far more from it than I could ever give back. Perhaps to my own credit, I fully recognize this.

Thank you so much for reading. It's difficult to express how much I appreciate it.

Wickliffe, Ohio
September 2023

Acknowledgements

To Terry and the children, who were already mentioned in the dedication but who are, after all, the 5 Kids and the 1 Wife.

To Robert and Kathryn Tennant, my parents, for allowing me to feel loved, always.

To Judi, Debbie and Mark, my siblings, for making the chronological gap between us feel so much smaller.

To my extended family for being good sports when their names get mentioned in the blog. That includes everyone from my nephew Mark and my father-in-law Tom to my brother-in-law Dave, my sister-in-law Chris, and my kids' significant others (Mark, Michael, Lyndsey and Austin), among a longer list of kith and kin.

To Brian Sooy for a deeply helpful tutorial on the world of self-publishing.

To Callie Bumba for forcing me to think visually and for designing this book's wonderful front and back covers.

To Catherine Williams for making these pages look far, far better than I ever could. Authors, get yourself a good interior book designer.

To Ron Kotar for graciously allowing me to use a wonderful photo he took of Jack conducting the high school band (you'll find it in the epilogue).

To everyone who has, over the years, been a regular reader of the blog. You endured several stops and starts on my part, but you always clicked through, you always read the posts, you always interacted, and you always reminded me there was a small but engaged audience on the other end of the keyboard. I can never thank you enough.

PARENTING

By now I thought I would have parenting figured out.
Of course, by now I also thought the Browns would
win a Super Bowl, so…

The world begins evaluating your children the moment they're born

Our family, September 2000, shortly after Melanie was born.

February 6, 2012: If you've ever had a baby – or, like me, have watched your wife have a baby – you're probably familiar with the Apgar score.

The Apgar score is a way for doctors to assess the health of a newborn. It takes into account things like pulse rate, muscle tone and breathing, and it's done on a scale of 1 to 10.

I can't remember the exact Apgar scores of my children, but I'm pretty sure they were all around 9 (there may have been one 8 in there, I don't know). What I do remember is that none of them got a 10.

In every instance, this genuinely offended me as a father. These kids were seconds old, dripping in goo and in some cases still physically attached to their mother through a slimy umbilical cord, and already someone was judging them ... and finding them lacking.

"Wait, why didn't my kid get a perfect score? What's wrong with her? She's beautiful and perfect, DO YOU HEAR ME? PERFECT!"

I was, of course, an idiot. The Apgar score obviously is not a measure of a baby's worth as a person, but right away I became The Overbearing Protective Father.

If one of my kids had received, say, a score of 5 or less, I guarantee my thought process would have been something like, "Oh no, there's something wrong with him. All the other kids are going to make fun of him. He'll have no confidence and won't be able to get into an elite kindergarten. That will put him on the 'normal track,' and Harvard and Princeton will never accept him. I've already failed as a parent."

(NOTE: If this sounds neurotic to you, it is. I'm a far mellower dad now than I was when we first had kids, though even then I mostly kept my insane thoughts to myself. Thankfully.)

I bring this up in the wake of Solo & Ensemble Contest, which we attended recently. For those who aren't band geeks, Solo & Ensemble Contest – or just "Contest," as it's commonly known – is an annual event in which instrumental and vocal students perform in front of judges, who give them ratings from 1 to 5 ... or actually "I to V," since they use Roman numerals.

Not every band kid participates in Contest, but a lot do. Terry and I did when we were in high school, so between that and the fact that their private lessons teachers would find it unacceptable if they didn't, Elissa and Chloe also endure the Contest experience each year.

What happens is that your band teacher or private instructor assigns you a piece to perform, usually something classical and challenging to play. Then you practice it for months in preparation for a single 10-minute period when you have to play it for a judge. The goal is to earn a "I" (superior) rating because … well, I don't know the "because." Really, until this moment, I never considered *why* this is done. To make you a better musician? To teach you something about the value of hard work and discipline? To humiliate you in front of others? I'll say yes, yes and yes.

The kids put a lot of work into the process, and it's always nerve-wracking when it's time to walk to the performance room and play your piece for evaluation. "Nerve-wracking," that is, for the parents. The kids get nervous, too, but *nothing* like the parents, believe me.

I hate the whole Contest experience because I'm afraid my kid will feel like a failure if he/she falls short of his/her goal. And since the kids have my nonsensical, stress-inducing tendency toward perfectionism, the goal for them is always a "I." Always. They're little overachievers, and I'm afraid they'll slit their wrists if they get anything less than the top score.

Honestly, I don't care if they get a "I" or not. I would like them to earn the highest rating, of course, but it's not that big a deal to me if they don't. But it IS a big deal to them, and I don't want them to feel bad. So I worry. And I get really nervous. And so does Terry.

When Elissa was playing her solo at Contest a couple of weeks ago, I glanced over at Terry and noticed she was doing the same thing I was doing: looking straight down toward the floor. I did it because it made the knot in my stomach even bigger if I looked at Elissa while she played. Terry did it because she figured eye contact would make Elissa more nervous. Our family is just one big, sensitive Ball of Nervous at Contest. What should be a fun experience instead shortens each of our life spans by five years.

I feel the same way at spelling bees. The whole thing is unpleasant for me. Really, any event in which my kid will be evaluated, judged, assessed and/or otherwise put up for appraisal makes my insides churn. I know it's good for them, but I don't like it.

Now Elissa is a senior on the verge of entering college, and the whole competition thing is even worse: What's your class rank? Your SAT score? Your ACT score? Your grades?

This Sunday she and two teammates will be taping an episode of "Academic Challenge" to air on Cleveland's WEWS-TV Channel 5 in the spring. They'll be up against two other schools, which means there will be a winning team and two losing teams. Get that? Only 33% of participants will succeed, while the other 67% will fail. That's the way it is, and either way my heart will be racing.

It makes me look forward 20 years into the future when we'll have grandchildren, and my kids will be the ones doing the worrying. Of course, I'll probably get even more nervous for the grandkids' events and competitions. Maybe I should just have the inevitable heart attack now and get it over with.

The necessary evil of Chuck E. Cheese

February 27, 2012: Jack got invited to a friend's birthday party at Chuck E. Cheese. You veteran parents know how this works: You go to Target, buy a gift in the toy department, wrap it, take your kid to the House of Cheese and either drop him/her off (if you're smart) or else agree to stay and help supervise.

My good friend Lenny Luscher once called Chuck E. Cheese "Babylon for kids," and I think that's pretty accurate. Contained within those four walls is every possible kid form of sin and vice … and, thanks to the addition of beer and wine to the menu, some for the adults, as well.

The rides and games vary by Chuck E. Cheese location, but there are at least three constants no matter which one you visit:

1. A jumbo-sized Habitrail in which kids crawl around and share germs with others their age

2. A variety of games that introduce them to gambling by offering tickets for the winners

3. Noise – lots and lots of noise

That last point is crucial. Do not go to Chuck E. Cheese thinking you're in for a relaxing time while your child eats pizza, ingests mass quantities of sugary soda and plays skee-ball. The Cheese

Experience is loud, and it's almost always uncomfortably hot. Little kids will constantly run into your knees like tiny Ndamukong Suhs, trying to get from one activity to the other. No matter how well you have trained your children, they will quickly conform to the pattern of obnoxious, rude behavior so favored by the tiny denizens of The Cheese.

And yet, I would argue the world needs Chuck E. Cheese. It wouldn't bother me if I never walked into one again, but it's my firm belief that there's a certain ying and yang between grown-ups and kids that needs to be maintained.

Think of it from a child's point of view. Ninety-five percent of the time, kids are forced to live, work and play in decidedly adult-oriented environments. Even when they're around other kids, like at school, they do it in a setting created and sustained by adults.

Chuck E. Cheese is one of the few places they can go that is entirely theirs. That fake Chuck E. Cheese band up on the stage? They love that. Seriously, they may not admit it, but listening to that animatronic band strike up a bluegrass version of "The Farmer in the Dell" for the 27th time in less than an hour is like scoring front-row seats to Led Zeppelin for them.

The games, the grimy ball pit, the noise ... this is paradise for small people. They can do what they want for as long as they want (or at least until the tokens run out), and no annoying grown-up is going to yell at them for being too loud or for having too much fun.

Trust me, this is a good thing. If we the people in charge were to take away their last 5% of freedom, they would revolt. There would be a full-scale kid revolution if we shut down Chuck E. Cheese and places like it. These kids (who already tend to be fast and agile) would be angry, and pre-adolescent anger is sufficiently powerful to destroy civilization as we know it.

The Chuck E. Cheese people understand this, which is why

they offer booze. They don't want you getting crazy ideas in your head about how their environment is probably damaging to your child's long-term mental health, so they offer up fairly low-cost Chardonnay and Budweiser to head you off. That nice little buzz not only gives you the stamina to endure the chaos, it also keeps you from setting fire to the place.

As parents and as a society, we need The Cheese.

We already hug our kids a little tighter

(NOTE: This post was written shortly after six students were shot at Chardon (Ohio) High School. Three died. Chardon is about a half hour east of us, and my niece was just feet away from the shooter when he opened fire.)

February 29, 2012: The last thing you want or need is 500 words from me about the Chardon High School shootings. Other than having a niece and nephew who are students there and who thankfully escaped safe and sound, the whole thing really has little to do with me.

And even if it did, what do I know? I'm not going to tell you anything new. I'm not going to give you any pearls of wisdom to make sense of the whole thing. I have no insights and little advice to offer.

But I will say this: What happened in Chardon on Monday morning in no way made me hug my kids any tighter or feel any more apprehensive about dropping them off for school. I'm no more worried for their safety today than I was last week.

Why? Because my approach to parenting has always been to operate at a consistent state of low-level panic. I don't show it very often (people will describe me as being "laid back" … I wish), but deep down, every day I run through a mental checklist of Things That Could Go Wrong for the Kids.

What if they get hit by a bus? What if they get into a fight?

PARENTING

What if someone picks on them? What if they fail a test?

And yes, what if some kid brings a gun to school? That's something that crosses my mind from time to time, because I live in Wickliffe, Ohio. We in Wickliffe dealt with our own school shooting back in 1994, five years before Columbine and long before school shootings became tragically commonplace.

A heroic custodian was killed and two staff members and a police officer were wounded, including my 8th-grade football coach, Mr. Grimm.

I didn't have kids in school at the time. In fact, my oldest daughter, Elissa, was only 7 months old. Nearly every day I would take her for an afternoon walk in the stroller so that she could get some fresh air and a little shuteye, and I could get some exercise.

We generally followed the same circular route, one that took us past Wickliffe Middle School. It was pretty nice for early November (an online weather almanac says the high in Cleveland that day was 57 degrees, though I seem to remember it being warmer). As we walked down Route 84 toward Lincoln Road, sirens suddenly came screaming from every direction. Police cars, fire trucks and ambulances from surrounding communities zoomed past, all of them turning down Lincoln Road toward the elementary and middle schools.

I didn't know what was happening at the time, but my first instinct as a parent was that it couldn't be good and that I should turn around and go home, so I did. When I got back to the house, I put Elissa down for a nap and turned on the TV. And there on CNN, for all the world to see, was a still photo of the middle school lobby, with glass and debris strewn on the floor after a lone gunman had come in and shot the place up.

Like I said, I had no older kids at the time, but I was shocked. I had attended that school. I had lived in this city my entire life to that point (and still do). There were the usual choruses of, "This is the last place you would expect something like this to happen," just as we heard over and over again about Chardon. It was terrible.

It's still terrible. It's terrible because you can't be a parent in this city and not have that memory burned somewhere into your mind. At some level of my consciousness, it's always there.

That's why I am no more on the lookout for things that could hurt my kids now than I've ever been before. When it happens that close to home, it never quite leaves you.

I hate that we live in a world like this. I hate that in addition to all of the natural worries I have as a father, there's always that incident hovering in the background. But it's the way things are, and it's something we deal with as parents.

As I type this, I'm wearing a red shirt and a red and black tie – Chardon's school colors – in what I hope is some feeble but meaningful gesture of support for the people there. Few if any of them will ever see it, and I suppose it's really more for myself than anything.

In a couple of weeks, things in Chardon will start to return to something approaching "normal." People will be back in their routines. Teachers and kids will return to classes, assemblies and school concerts. The TV people will finally leave, surfacing once a year on Feb. 27th to mark the anniversary of the shootings. And slowly but surely, as it always does, life will go on.

But I'll tell you one thing.: The memory of it will never go away completely. The parents of Chardon, Ohio, will always carry it with them, and perhaps subconsciously they'll continue hugging their kids a little tighter and worrying about them a little more every day for the rest of their lives. It's just what happens. It's heartbreaking, but it's what happens.

When a child chunders

March 3, 2012: I applaud you single parents. I don't begin to understand how you do what you do, but you do it, and for that you deserve all the credit in the world.

There are certain parenting situations that, to my mind, almost require two people to handle. Here I'm thinking specifically of those times when a child throws up in the middle of the night.

All of the kids' rooms are upstairs in our house, while the master bedroom is on the ground floor. Therefore, Terry and I never actually hear it when someone blows chunks in their bed. Instead, we are jolted awake when they come into our room and say those horrifying words: "Mommy? Daddy? I threw up."

Whenever this happens, I try to lay perfectly still for at least five seconds. My dearest hope in the world is that it's all a dream and I can fall back asleep peacefully. But it never, ever happens that way. It's always real, and Terry and I throw off the soft, warm covers to head upstairs and survey the damage.

This is when we fall into our assigned roles. We are a top-notch Puke Response Team. Neither of us has to say anything like, "OK, you do this and I'll do that." We just know.

Terry's job is to attend to the Vomiting Victim. Are they OK? Do they feel like they're going to throw up again? What is the condition of their pajamas? Do they need to change? Did any of it splatter into their hair? Do they need comforting? Terry runs through this mental checklist in about two seconds. It's beautiful to watch.

I, meanwhile, am in charge of crime scene clean-up. This generally involves three things:

1. Cleaning as much of the excess vomit – solid and liquid – off all surfaces with which it has come into contact, usually the bed or the floor.

2. Taking soiled sheets and clothes (which Terry will have quickly removed from the child and passed on to me) downstairs to the laundry room so I can throw them into the washer.

3. Dealing with any vomit stains on the carpet. On my way back up from the laundry room, I'll grab a bottle of spray cleaner from under the kitchen sink and apply it to all areas of the carpet that have been violated by barf. As I'm waiting for the cleaner to soak in and do its job, I will sometimes fall asleep as I stand there in the child's room. This has happened several times.

Having taken care of the immediate needs of the little horker, Terry must now make the decision as to where the child will spend the rest of the night. If they seem to feel OK, and her motherly intuition tells her it's safe, she will throw a comforter over the now-stripped mattress and let the kid sleep in their own bed. If there seems to be more imminent danger of pukage, she will put the comforter on the living room floor next to the couch and have the child sleep there. In either case, a bucket is kept close by the would-be upchucker in case of a repeat incident.

By this time I have sponged up any floor stains and returned the cleaning materials to their proper place. We meet back at the bed and discuss vomit-related strategy for the rest of the night. Then we put our heads down and are both asleep in seconds.

All of this happens quickly, but it's exhausting. It interrupts the whole sleep-cycle thing and takes away several precious minutes of shuteye. And that's with two of us on the case. I can't imagine doing this myself, yet single parents do just that. You all deserve a medal.

And a clean set of child-sized bed sheets, too.

The art of dadness

March 26, 2012: It's tricky being a father in the 21st century.

Guys of my generation are influenced by two very different styles of parenting: On one hand, most of us had fathers who were of the old school. They were generally good dads, but they left the majority of parenting duties to their wives. Their involvement in the child-rearing process was fairly limited to serving as procreators, disciplinarians and financial backers. And in some cases, not much else.

On the other hand, we ourselves are raising kids at a time when fathers are (happily) expected to be far more hands-on. Unlike many of our dads, we were right there to witness the birth of our children, which as Sting once very aptly said makes the whole thing "much more bloody and profound."

In that alone we are sometimes more closely connected to our kids from the very start than our fathers might have been.

We are also rightly expected to take part in all day-to-day aspects of parenting. This is eminently fair but also sometimes a little challenging.

The only role models we had for this were our moms, since our dads were so often out working or doing other manly things that kept them absent from the minutiae of having kids. Consequently, a lot of us follow our mothers' lead when it comes to parenting style.

Women, for the most part, are pretty understanding of this

Jack and Coach Daddy, 2012

ongoing conflict in our lives and as a gender have been remarkably tolerant of our fatherly shortcomings. One side effect is that the bar is set fairly low for modern dads, and anything we do right is met with cheers and applause.

Seriously, it's not that difficult to be considered a good dad nowadays. You show up to little league games, change a few diapers, stay home and watch the kids when your wife goes out and, presto, you're suddenly a candidate for Father of the Year.

I've always thought the standards should be a lot higher than that. If we're going to be what we're supposed to be as dads, I think someone needs to push us a little harder.

Speaking of watching the kids, you know what has always bothered me? When someone sees me alone with my children and asks whether I'm "babysitting" them. As if they don't actually belong to me and I'm just pretending to be a parent for a bit while my wife is out shopping. The two irksome implications of this question are:

- The responsibility for watching the kids really falls on my wife and I'm graciously offering to do her job for her.

- I'm incompetent and can't be trusted to do this for too long.

In all fairness, I don't think people who ask whether I'm "babysitting" my kids mean anything negative by it. Usually they're of an older generation that simply had a different approach to parenting. But it still bothers me.

I am of the opinion that fathers are valuable. That's not at all to say that single mothers can't raise quality kids. They do it all the time, and they amaze me. (I know some great single fathers, too.)

I'm just saying a dad brings something to the equation that's difficult for a parent of the other gender to match, just as a father on his own can't give his kids everything a mother can.

I had a great dad. He was goofy, and he had his quirks and faults, but not for a second – not for a single second – did I ever doubt he loved me and cared for my well-being. The effect of that simple fact on my life has been immeasurably positive, and I want my kids to enjoy the same thing.

Because let's face it: We can't rely on moms to tell stupid jokes, make bad puns, wear hideously mismatched outfits in public and fall asleep on the couch with their hands in their pants. These are time-honored dad traditions, and by God, I will do everything in my power to uphold them.

The Lazy Person's Guide to Parent-Teacher Conferences

April 4, 2012: At least once a year, we parents are summoned to our child's school to participate in the ritual known as parent-teacher conferences. Ostensibly, the idea here is to find out what your child is learning, how well they're learning it, how they're behaving, and how mom and dad can help the educational process along.

I have no time for any of that. I know I should be deeply engaged in my child's school experience, but I'm really only concerned with three things when I attend a parent-teacher conference:

1. Is my kid getting an "A" in your class?

2. If not, in what specific area is the little ingrate falling behind so I can use that as leverage the next time he/she wants something?

3. Are you inclined to tell me how awesome my son/daughter is? If so, I will give you one minute to expound on this thesis, after which I will likely get bored.

Again, I know I'm not modeling the best parenting behavior here, but I *am* being realistic. My life is busy. So is yours. I'm just looking for bottom-line information.

PARENTING

If there's anything in which I take pride, it's item #2 above. Well, not the part in which I blackmail my children based on their school performance, but rather the first part about how I automatically assume it's my kid's fault (and not the teacher's) if they're not doing well in a particular class. I would love to say my little angels can do no wrong, but the reality is that most of the time when their grades slip, it's their own fault. And generally the reason is that they were too lazy to complete a certain assignment or to come in early to get help from the teacher.

And while we're on the subject, God bless teachers. I know the majority of you teachers love what you do, and as a consequence I love *you* for it. I'm not sure I could deal with whiny, misbehaving children all day AND have to listen to parents complain that I'm the reason their little darling is getting a "D." Kudos to all of you.

My kids had some wonderful teachers through the years, but my approach to parent-teacher conferences was always about efficiency.

My favorite approach to parent-teacher conferences is the one they use at our local middle and high schools. You walk into the cafeteria where the teachers are seated at different tables around

25

the room. It's like a teacher buffet, and you can pick and choose the ones you want to talk to, and in what order. Whoever came up with this idea is a genius.

We have five kids attending the school system from which my wife and I both graduated, so to say we're familiar with the people and personalities involved is risking gross understatement. We spend a good chunk of our conference time just chatting with the teachers about everything EXCEPT our children.

When we do get around to discussing the topic at hand, it doesn't take that long. Because like I said, I'm just looking for cause, effect and outcome. Give me the grade. If it's an "A," there's not much more we need to talk about. If it's not, you tell me why and I'll take it from here. Case closed, we can all go home.

Sometimes, though, you'll come across the sort of teacher I call the Curriculum Whisperer. This is the person who wants to tell you every detail about what your child is learning in their class. While this can actually be interesting, I keep glancing at my watch and thinking that if the explanation of how one goes about teaching fifth-graders basic economics is this boring, imagine how the actual class must be.

I also enjoy the Teacher Who Isn't 100% Sure Who Your Kid Is. This doesn't happen too often to us, given that we know so many of the teachers and have lived in this school district forever, but it's a lot of fun when it does.

We'll approach a teacher and sit down at their table, and the teacher will give us a blank look and say, "Hiiiiiiii, uhhhhh...." And then there will be this awkward silence during which they're hoping we'll either identify ourselves or the name of our child will suddenly pop into their head. I usually make them sweat it out for a few seconds before I finally relent and say, "Hi, we're Scott and Terry. We're Jared's parents." It's cruel, I know, but I'm trying to squeeze whatever entertainment I can out of this activity.

Once we get home, we'll give a debriefing to the child or children we just spent an hour discussing. Generally speaking, the news will largely be positive and we all move on. But when there's an issue to be addressed or a particular grade to be bolstered, you can be sure *somebody* is going to be doing extra chores to make up for it. That is, of course, if they ever want Daddy to open his wallet again when they're looking to go to the movies with their friends.

The end of the innocence (but not yet)

May 8, 2012: I came home from work the other night in a hurry. It was a little before 6:30, and we had our end-of-the-season party for Jack's soccer team starting at 7. I'm the coach, so I wanted to get there on time.

As I rushed into our bedroom to change clothes, I saw Jack sitting at the computer playing a game. He turned around when I came in and you could see the twinkle in his eyes. What he said made me want to hug him.

"I'm so excited for our party!" he burst out, and you could see he meant it, too. "I told my friends at school all about it!"

These end-of-the-season parties are, you understand, not elaborate affairs. I reserve a pavilion at one of our city parks, and the parents and kids gather there to munch on pizza and desserts, drink lemonade, and enjoy one last evening together before going their separate ways for the summer.

We also have a little program where I call the kids up one at a time, talk about the season they had, and present each with a signed certificate awarding them with a unique title. For example, one is deemed "Most Valuable Offensive Player," while another might be "Ms. Versatility" (for the girl who plays all of the positions well) or "Most Improved Boy."

I gave Jack the "Iron Man Award," which I bestow each year on the boy who plays the hardest, always gets up when he's knocked down, and gives his all each and every time he's on the field. We have the "Iron Woman Award," too.

Jack didn't know he was going to get that particular honor. All he knew was that he was going to be in a place where he and his soccer friends could eat junk food together, play on the playground, and just enjoy being around each other. And he was openly, genuinely excited at this prospect.

I'm sure there was a time in my life when that would have thrilled me, too, but it has been so long I can't remember. My 6-year-old couldn't wait to get to the park, and my heart broke for him.

That may not seem like a heartbreaking moment, I realize. And right now it's not. But I know that in just a few short years, getting excited about a soccer pizza party is going to be the furthest thing from cool, and that the 11-year-old version of Jack will never walk around school telling his friends how excited he is about it, lest he run the risk of being made fun of.

I understand that, and I certainly lived it myself many years ago. But part of me still wants to hug him. Part of me wants to hold him tight for just a few seconds and whisper in his ear, "Don't ever, ever lose that enthusiasm. Don't ever let anyone tell you what's worth getting excited about and what isn't. Don't ever let the rest of the world dictate to you what's cool. Because you know what, buddy? You're right … soccer pizza parties ARE awesome."

Come to think of it, I *will* tell him that. And he'll agree with me, I suspect, though there's probably no avoiding the I-just-want-to-fit-in-and-not-be-different years that are coming. Virtually all of us go through them. The trick is coming back full circle and eventually allowing ourselves to be whatever we want to be, regardless of what anyone else thinks or says.

That night, if only for the 90 minutes the pizza party lasted, that was the lesson I learned from my little boy.

It's not my fault, says the youngster before me

May 14, 2012: I'm fairly certain my children will all end up being lawyers. Good ones, too. As far as they're concerned, none of them has ever actually been guilty of doing anything wrong.

It is not uncommon for me to have conversations that go like this:

ME: So let me get this straight. You're about to get on the bus without having written your English paper, which is due in 30 minutes because you have that class first period, and this happened DESPITE the fact that your mother and I each reminded you of it eight times last night?

CHILD: Yes.

ME: And further, it is your contention that this circumstance is actually not your fault in any way?

CHILD: Yes.

ME: I see. While I doubt I really want to hear the answer, can you enlighten me as to why, pray tell, it is NOT your fault the English paper wasn't written?

CHILD: Mommy didn't wake me up early to write it.

ME: That's it? That's your reason? Did you ASK Mommy to wake you up early so you could write it?

CHILD: No, but she should have known.

ME: Really? So your mother should, for all intents and purposes, have anticipated your stunning irresponsibility and should have taken it upon herself – without you at least having made the request – to wake you up early to write a paper that should have been written a week ago? Is that what you're telling me here?

CHILD (*entirely straight-faced*): Well, yeah. Why is this so hard for you to understand?

ME: <*speechless*>

The thing is, they say this stuff with such conviction and force, they almost end up winning me over. I start to think, "Oh well, now I see. I guess I'll just write a note asking the teacher to excuse him from the assignment because his parents were negligent."

Fortunately, the forces of common sense generally prevail in my mind and I can only wonder where I went wrong with these children. Because you see, they BELIEVE what they're saying. They perceive nothing wrong with leaving messes for their mother to clean up because, clearly, that's her JOB, right? She's their personal maidservant, and if she can't see that, well, then the problem is clearly with Mommy and not with them.

I will walk into the basement and find empty plates and cups left by someone who was probably down there earlier in the day (or even the night before) watching TV and having a snack. I will ascertain who this person is, go upstairs, and order them into the basement to clean up the mess. They'll do it, but only after giving me a look that says, "You want me to do what? Clean up after myself? Well, that's just unacceptable. What am I, your slave? You should have asked Mommy to do it."

Terry, for her part, has done very well over the years in that she has not murdered any of her children. Believe me, she may not admit it, but I know the thought has crossed her mind. I've seen that look in her eyes. It's a look you don't want to receive from anyone, let alone your mother. It's a look that says the electric chair may very well be worth it if only for the chance to strangle a 14-year-old.

In the interest of fairness, I should note that my children really are good kids, despite their father's influence. And this sort of thing doesn't happen all the time. But it happens just often enough that Terry and I will have serious conversations that include the sentence, "Maybe having five kids wasn't the best idea."

My only real hope, at this point, is that we can get through the next 15 years or so without Terry causing serious bodily harm to one of them. Keep Terry felony-free, that's pretty much all I'm aiming for between now and, say, 2030. If we can get there, I'll have done my job.

The numbing realization that no parent really has any idea what they're doing

One sure sign of my parental incompetence was a tendency to fire off highly combustible model rockets in the presence of my young children.

June 11, 2012: Howie Mandel once said something that still resonates with me.

This was when Howie was doing stand-up comedy back in the mid-80s. And he had hair. And he wasn't so OCD about people touching him. And he used to stretch a surgical glove over his head and blow it up with his nose, which I still find hilarious because I'm an extremely simple man who will laugh at almost anything.

Howie and his wife had just had their first child. He mentioned that sometimes he would stop in the middle of whatever he was doing and say to himself, "I'm someone's DAD." The point being that he was just a big goofball, and someone in authority had clearly messed up if he, Howie Mandel, was allowed to be the father of a tiny human being.

I'm willing to bet there's not a parent alive who has not felt something similar. You can read all the books you want. You can babysit all the kids you want. You can take all the classes you want. When you bring that baby home from the hospital for the first time and there are no longer any nurses around to take the little rugrat away whenever you feel the least bit sleepy, *that's* when reality sets in.

It starts as a low-grade panic somewhere deep in your stomach. Then it gets worse as you realize this is actually happening, that YOU are the one ultimately responsible for the well-being of this impossibly small creature.

You think to yourself, "This isn't good. I am not the least bit qualified for this job. I am a Grade A screw-up who can barely remember to change the filter in my fish tank, and suddenly I have to feed, dress and otherwise oversee the upbringing of another person? No, this is not good."

I remember when Terry and I brought Elissa home from the hospital. We were dead tired (she more so than me, for obvious reasons). Elissa was sleeping peacefully, as I recall, but when we unloaded everything from the car and laid her down in her little bassinet, we realized we had no idea what to do next. Not a clue.

I think we just sort of sat and stared at each other for a minute. Then we turned on the TV. Whenever Elissa made any sort of noise, we both jumped up and checked on her to see what was wrong.

That night, our first as parents in our own home, was terrible. Elissa continued making the sort of small, ultimately inconsequential noises newborns do. Every time she did, one or both of us would jerk our heads up and wonder if we needed to go get her.

By the next morning, we were wrecks. Tired, disheveled, and most of all crushingly disheartened at the prospect of spending the next several hundred nights doing the same thing.

But somehow, we got through. Night by night we survived. We developed a little routine where I would get up first whenever Elissa awoke (which admittedly wasn't often compared with a lot of babies), change her diaper, and bring her to Terry for breastfeeding.

Slowly but surely, things got easier. We managed to keep Elissa alive long enough for Chloe to be born. And then Jared. And then Melanie. And finally Jack. Somewhere along the way we learned what it meant to be parents. We're still learning, in fact.

I hope Howie eventually did, too.

Boosting the confidence of your less-confident kids

March 13, 2013: I have five children, and they have five different personalities. Which is good, really. It would be boring to have five little carbon copies running around the house (NOTE: If you don't know what carbon copies are, I'm going to dock you 10 points for making me feel old.)

If there's one thing the majority of my kids share, it's healthy self-esteem. Terry and I have always tried to foster in them a strong sense of their own unique abilities and positive character traits. I

The beautiful Miss Melanie as a high school senior (by which point she had gained much of the confidence she previously lacked)

would say that's true of 80% of the children. (For you humanities majors, I should explain that means four of the five.)

The holdout is Melanie. Or "little Melanie," as I've always called her. She's 12 now and taller than a lot of her friends, so the "little" part is misleading. It stems from the five-year period in which Mel was the baby of the family before Jack was born. I always think of her as "little Melanie."

Melanie is a wonderfully talented, smart, beautiful girl. She is already an accomplished musician, actor and soccer player, and one of those kids for whom the sky is very obviously the limit.

Not that Mel used to believe any of that about herself. For a long time, she was held back by the belief that she wasn't very good at anything. This is common in a significant subset of kids, but it's especially prevalent in girls.

Try as we might to convince Melanie of her own worth, she would consistently doubt herself. At one point, Terry was actually making her repeat this self-validating mantra: "I am a smart, beautiful, confident woman." Really. She would have Mel say it aloud five or 10 times in a row in the hope that the child would start to believe it.

I've noticed over the last several months, ever since Melanie entered 6th grade, that her confidence seems to be on the upswing, which is a relief. She still doesn't have a real sense for just how good she is (and will be) at a lot of things, but I think she's trending in the right direction.

Which brings me to today's question: How do you go about boosting the confidence of kids who, for whatever reason, don't really believe in themselves? It took us awhile to figure it out with Melanie, but let me suggest five approaches that may work:

1. **Let them know they're worthy ... and they're loved**
   I was a parent for quite a long time before I realized just how

impactful the things we say to our kids can be. Sting penned this line in a song about the death of his father: "This indifference was my invention, when everything I did sought your attention." There's a lot of truth there. Yes, young people are very much influenced by their peers. But ultimately, it's the words of our parents that stick with us. As often as possible, they need to be positive words of affirmation.

2. **But don't go overboard**
The thing is, kids are smart enough to know the difference between genuine, heartfelt praise and sugar-coated platitudes. They do need constructive criticism when it's warranted. Don't feel you have to laud them 75 times a day for every little thing they do ("Good job flushing the toilet, Johnny!")

3. **Play to their strengths**
Almost invariably, your child will gravitate toward the things at which she shows some level of ability or aptitude. This is natural (you probably do it, too). To the extent you can, encourage them to pursue these interests at higher and higher levels. This not only creates a sense of accomplishment, it also helps them figure out what they might want to do with their lives once they leave your house. And trust me, one day they will actually leave.

4. **Challenge them**
At the same time, the kid has to learn how to fail. Losing is as important as (and I might argue *more* important than) winning when you're growing up. Life's tough. They either learn to accept that fact now or they grow up to be whiny, dependent, reactive people. Ironically, the better they learn to handle failure, the more confident they'll become. I'm not quite sure how or why that works, but it does.

PARENTING

5. **Create a safe, loving home environment**

Kids who don't feel safe or loved at home are at the greatest risk of developing poor self-esteem, and therefore low self-confidence. If a child doesn't see his/her home as a safe haven in which family members are supportive, encouraging and understanding, they're going to be less willing to take risks or try something new. Like most things, it all starts at home. You as the parent are the one who sets the tone there. Don't ever forget that.

Remember when kids used to have their summers free?

June 12, 2013: I will try my best not to turn this into a "hey, things were a lot better when I was younger" post, because I'm not someone who generally thinks that way.

But I will say this about the experience of being a kid now vs. the days when I was a kid in the 70s and 80s:

Back when I was a lad, summer vacation meant … well, it meant "summer vacation." It meant you had half of June and all of July and August to yourself to do with as you pleased.

Apart from family vacations and the occasional little league baseball game (which occurred, what, twice a week?), you were on your own.

And it was glorious.

Of course, being a kid, you absolutely took for granted the whole concept of waking up on a warm summer morning and having nothing but a blank slate of a day ahead of you.

Only when the first day of school rolled around did you really appreciate what you had lost.

That first day of school, by the way, was always after Labor Day. Always. Now my kids start new school years in mid-August, seemingly 20 minutes or so after the previous one ends.

Anyway, we had gigantic chunks of unstructured time in the summer months, and we used them to engage in what was, for me, a lot of fun stuff.

We played sports and games outside. We played our Atari 2600 systems inside.

We rode our bikes. We went to the city pool.

We set up failed lemonade stands. We set off firecrackers that one of us had somehow gotten our hands on.

We watched TV. We played more Atari.

You probably have a similar list from your own childhood.

The point is, we did a lot of things without interference from (or really the need for) adults. Both the kids and grown-ups were just fine with this system.

Then two things happened that started the whole thing spinning out of control.

One was the specialization of sports. By that I mean the drive to make kids better at their chosen sport through an influx of summer camps, clinics, practices, conditioning sessions, etc.

Doesn't matter what your sport is: baseball, football, basketball, hockey, soccer, lacrosse. Whatever. If you're a kid and you play it, there are programs designed solely to expose you to that sport year-round.

With that also came the creeping influence of club sports, travel programs, Junior Olympic teams, and so forth. Those have become all-consuming for families across the nation.

Not that I think there's anything intrinsically wrong with these activities. If you choose to participate in them, and if it makes your child happy, by all means, go for it.

But the unintended side effect of these leagues and programs is that kids who just play sports for fun, who will never receive college athletic scholarships, suddenly find themselves pressured to join. You either participate in the travel program in the summer or else you don't play when the actual sports season rolls around in fall or spring.

Well, that's OK, you might say. Kids like that can just join a no-pressure rec league.

Which would be fine, except cities and leagues in many places have taken their limited resources and directed them toward the travel and premier-level programs, leaving rec programs to rot on the vine with inferior equipment and few trained coaches.

That is, if the rec-level sport still exists at all. Many have just disappeared altogether.

The result is an all-or-nothing, travel-league-or-bust approach that alienates the average kid. So, rather than be left out, youngsters will often submit to the pressure of travel sports, and suddenly their calendars (summer and otherwise) fill up with practices, games and skill sessions that leave little time for any real relaxation.

The other thing that precipitated this trend is that overworked parents have started implementing structure in the lives of kids who didn't necessary need more of it.

Parents have always felt some degree of guilt over the amount of time they spend (or don't spend) with their children. Now, with magazine articles, TV psychiatrists and authors constantly reminding them just how slack they are in the parenting department, moms and dads try to compensate by exposing Junior to a wealth of new experiences through lessons, classes and seminars of every kind.

Every. Kind.

Many kids today need an administrative assistant just to keep track of their schedules. I had two things on my summer schedule when I was growing up:

8 a.m. – Get out of bed. Go find friends and commence day's activities.

9 p.m. – Come in when I was called and go to bed. Repeat cycle the next day.

And I guess I turned out OK. For what that's worth.

You don't hear many kids complaining about this turn of events, and I'm guessing it's because they don't know any different. They've never had unstructured summers, so they don't know what they're missing.

I'll tell you what they're missing.

A lot.

But maybe that's just the product of the undisciplined mind of a guy who spent his childhood summers playing in his friends' backyards. What do I know?

I would have been fine with a house full of daughters, but sons are nice, too

March 30, 2015: My wife birthed five babies, and we didn't find out the gender of any of them before they were born. Let me say three things about that:

1. **Just because we did it that way doesn't mean I think anyone else has to do it that way.** It was our choice for us. Your choice may be different, which is totally fine. Why do some people feel their way is always The Right Way and that everyone must follow their lead? Or, conversely, that if someone makes a choice different from theirs, that's automatically a threat or a challenge to them? In most cases for most things, it's OK that we can make different choices and co-exist. There doesn't have to be a "right" and a "wrong."

2. **My gender guess was incorrect every time.** I went 0 for 5 in my kid gender predictions. That's like flipping a coin five times and failing to call it correctly even once. It's far from impossible, and it may be even more probable than I think, but still…how did I not get it right just one time?

3. **We had two girls before we had our first boy, and while I love my sons, I would have been fine with a house full**

of daughters. It turns out having sons is great and I love it, but by Baby #3, I was comfortable with all aspects of having daughters. Well, "all aspects" meaning those things pertaining to having daughters ages 4 and almost 2, which is how old Elissa and Chloe were when Jared was born. They're relatively uncomplicated at that age and I felt I had reached a certain level of understanding with them.

For example, I could change a girl's diaper in seconds. I had a pattern down. A system, if you will. Then suddenly God threw a boy into the mix and ... wow. My wiping technique had to change drastically.

You can count on one hand the number of places on a baby girl where poop is likely to be found. But a boy? Suddenly there were folds on top of folds, and my Boy Diaper Changing Time ended up being roughly double what my Girl Diaper Changing Time was. It was traumatic at first.

Then there were girl clothes and hair ribbons and stuff. I learned how they all worked, and by the third kid I was somewhat confident with them. Then along comes a male child and I had a whole set of new stuff to learn. It wasn't hard, but again, it took me out of my Kid Comfort Zone.

I also liked the idea that, when the girls became teenagers, I could refer them to their mother for all questions that might be characterized as tricky, hair-raising, or feminine hygiene-related. But with boys, *I* was suddenly going to be the one with the answers. That was alarming.

In the end, I love having kids of both sexes. It gives you a whole new perspective on people, personalities and parenting. And it contributes greatly to what is already a fairly high level of chaos in my house, which I honestly wouldn't trade for anything.

But had God decided to bless me with five daughters, you would not hear me complaining. Daughters are, broadly speaking, funny, considerate, loving and just a delight to have around the house. I love being a father of girls.

Boys, however, also have their advantages. Again speaking very generally and no doubt stereotyping, boys tend to be less emotional, less dramatic, and more apt to talk about sports. A lot of girls are like that, too, but as I said, I'm generalizing. There's something to be said for having that boy element in your life when you're a dad.

In the end, we have to accept whatever nature gives us in terms of kid gender, but I think it's better if we accept it willingly, with a smile on our collective parenting faces. You may want that first kid to be a certain sex, but it's going to be what it's going to be and you're charged with raising it no matter what. So just roll with it, baby.

Also, you first-time parents should feel free to see me if you want a diaper-changing lesson. After three girls, two boys and thousands of diapers, I'm telling you, I'm a virtuoso.

What I miss and what I don't miss about having babies in the house

Elissa and me, 1994

May 15, 2015
WHAT I MISS: The free food and drink they stock in a refrigerator at the hospital specially for dads. That was awesome.
WHAT I DON'T MISS: Gallons and gallons of breast milk (frozen and otherwise) in our refrigerator at home.

WHAT I MISS: Lying down with a baby fast asleep on my shoulder.
WHAT I DON'T MISS: Lying down and wanting desperately to sleep with a baby who won't stop crying on my shoulder.

WHAT I MISS: Pooh Bear videos.
WHAT I DON'T MISS: Barney videos. (I was never anti-Barney, but a person can admittedly only take so much.)

WHAT I MISS: The Diaper Genie. What an ingenious invention.
WHAT I DON'T MISS: The Diaper Genie when it was full and needed emptying. The smell inside that thing was debilitating. One whiff and you were unable to do much of anything (including maintaining consciousness) for five full minutes.

WHAT I MISS: Freshly bathed babies.
WHAT I DON'T MISS: Actually bathing babies.

WHAT I MISS: The excitement of pregnancy and the impending arrival of a new addition to the family, made even more exciting by the fact that I wasn't the one who had to carry the little demon around in my abdomen for 9+ months.
WHAT I DON'T MISS: Getting home from the hospital with the baby and remembering that newborns are an insane amount of work.

WHAT I MISS: Setting up the playpen, knowing it was going to give you some hands-free time.

WHAT I DON'T MISS: Taking down the playpen, knowing I would either have to lug it somewhere when we left the house or set it up again 15 minutes later because we were already tired of holding the baby again.

WHAT I MISS: First smiles, first laughs, first words, first steps.

WHAT I DON'T MISS: First projectile vomiting, first teething, first non-breast milk poo, first tantrum.

WHAT I MISS: Watching my wife turn into a superhero of organization and energy as she cared for first one, then two, then three, then four, then five kids while I went off to work every day and basically abandoned her.

WHAT I DON'T MISS: Watching my wife dissolve into a puddle of tears and exhaustion when she was pretty sure she couldn't do it anymore (NOTE: She always got through it anyway because, as mentioned above, she's a superhero.)

Should you have another child? Here's my advice.

June 3, 2015: No.

Ha ha, just kidding! Sort of!

We have five children, all of whom are wonderful and a joy and a constant source of pride, and all of whom also occasionally frustrate me to the brink of homicide.

Right? You parents know what I'm talking about. Most of the time they're awesome. One of the best things that ever happened to you. Other times you want to strangle them.

That's the dichotomy of parenting: Deep, intense love intermingled with periodic criminal rage.

"I just love you so much. You're so wonderful and the best daughter anyone could ask for and ... wait, did you just leave your granola bar wrapper on the floor again? Yes, you did. PICK IT UP. PICK IT UP NOW! HOW MANY TIMES DO I HAVE TO TELL YOU NOT TO DO THAT? WHY ARE YOU SO BRAIN DAMAGED?!? PICK IT UP NOW! NOW! NOW!"

And so on.

Single-kid parents sometimes worry they could never love a second child as much as they do their ever-so-perfect first one. Which is wrong. If you have a second child (or a third child, or a fourth child...), your capacity for love will grow proportionately. I don't know how it works, but it does.

So don't worry about that part of it. Worry about the bills. I know that's a Dad Thing to Say, but seriously, multiple kids mean multiple expenses.

Like car insurance. If you have a toddler, the last thing on your mind is car insurance. Trust me, though, it will be an issue for you one day very soon.

Car insurance is expensive no matter who you are. Try getting coverage for a 16-year-old boy. Or an 18-year-old girl who has had a couple of accidents. Your premiums will have more digits than you even knew existed.

"Make the kids pay for insurance themselves," you say. Which I would do if they didn't have to go to school and instead had 30-40 hours a week available to work and earn the requisite cash.

So there's that.

And college. There's college. Presumably you'll want your children to pursue some form of post-secondary education. As you may have heard, college is a wee bit expensive.

As are clothes, food, housing and everything else the law (for whatever reason) requires you to provide for your children.

You need to take that stuff into account.

Another important factor? Your age. People are different, and we all have different levels of energy. But as you may have figured out from your first kid or two, having a baby is exhausting. Doing it in your 20s or even your early to mid-30s can be a whole lot different from doing it in your late 30s and 40s.

If you're pushing middle age – or if you're already there – you need to consider what having a baby will do to you. Even a baby that sleeps through the night. Babies in general sap a lot of energy from their parents. If you're cool with that, OK. I just want to make sure you're aware.

One last thing: If you decide to venture into large family territory, which I define as four kids or more, then understand that people will look at you funny. They'll assume you're Mormon or Evangelical or angling to get your own reality TV show or something. They'll say things like, "You know what causes that, right?" (NOTE: The correct reply to that is, "Yes, but look at me. My wife can't resist me, and if we're being honest, neither can yours.")

As a father of what nowadays passes for a large family, I can say you will become a borderline outcast from society. Few people will want you to visit their home for fear that your family will wreck the place. They'll make assumptions about you and your motivations and the amount of time you're able to spend with your children. Ignore them. You need to save your energy for walking around the house picking up discarded granola bar wrappers anyway.

WHY did you have kids?

February 1, 2016: No one has ever asked me this, so it only now occurs to me that I have no good answer to the question of why Terry and I had kids in the first place.

Why DID we have kids? And why five? I don't know that there was much conscious thought on either point. There was, frankly, a certain element of, "Well, we're married. We're young. Having kids is what you're supposed to do next."

But who says that's what you're supposed to do next? God, I guess. "Be fruitful and multiply" and all that. It's certainly not a requirement for living a happy and fulfilling life. Lots and lots of people are childless and perfectly content (or "child-free," as many like to say, as if having kids is some sort of disease … which for them it may well seem to be).

Beyond the "life momentum" thing, though, why have kids? What prompts someone to do that? I think there's a certain level of vanity to it. It's the biological equivalent of saying, "You know what? I'm a pretty good person. The world would be a better place if there were a few more people running around who look and act just like me."

NOTE TO WOULD-BE PARENTS: It doesn't always work that way. Your children may resemble one or both of you, but there's no guarantee they'll act the way you want them to act. I got lucky. Or I should say I was blessed. I happen to have ended up with good kids, due mostly to the tireless efforts of Terry to civilize the little beasts.

There's probably also a degree of curiosity to it. "I wonder what it would be like to have a baby. Or a toddler. Or an adolescent. Or a teenager. Or a young adult. Or all of the above." Unfortunately, the only way to answer these questions is to experience actual parenthood. If you happen to find you're not particularly good at it, or that it doesn't suit you, you're kind of stuck with the kid. Chalk it up to child protection laws and societal norms and whatnot.

Financially, kids can be a huge drain, though the U.S. tax code is written such that they serve as valuable deductions when you're filling out the ol' Form 1040. In the end, though, you spend far more money on them than you ever get back.

Truly, the payoff to having kids is intangible. I've written about it many times and would never, ever change a thing about the decisions Terry and I have made when it comes to having children. It is an incredible experience that has made me a far better person. Why did we have kids? I guess I don't know for sure. But the rewards are amazing.

Five things I want to tell my son on this, the day of his high school graduation

Jared, graduation day, 2017

May 23, 2017: Tonight, my son Jared graduates from high school, the third of our children to do so. Three down, two to go.

I will tell you I'm not pleased with the way this post turned out. I earnestly believe everything I'm trying to tell my son below, but none of it came out quite right.

Maybe that's because, while many life lessons are universal, the way we each learn and experience them is unique. So that even as I describe my own thoughts around a particular nugget of wisdom, I'm acutely aware that Jared's perspective on it is likely to be a bit different.

So I guess this list isn't perfect. No list of supposedly transcendent life lessons ever is. I hope the boy accepts it in the flawed-yet-sincere spirit in which it is offered.

Jared, we bought you a laptop for graduation, and now here's the gift that comes without a receipt:

1. **You've got to try even when you don't feel like trying:** Whatever you do, whether it's a job or a marriage or anything else important in life, you have to be present and you have to be actively engaged. That means showing up and really trying. Every day. Sometimes that's going to be easy. Sometimes it won't. You often hear it said of pitchers in baseball that they "just don't have it today," yet many times they stay in the game and "battle." They may not feel great, they may not feel motivated. But they have a job to do, so they do it. Even when they don't feel like doing it. That's the essence of being a responsible adult: You show up and you work hard every time without exception.

2. **Feeling sorry for yourself is tempting, but it will get you nowhere:** Sometimes you're going to feel like everything and everyone is against you. You can safely allow yourself to feel that way for maybe 15 minutes. Then you need to move on.

Seriously, you need to get over it and move on. Not everything is going to go your way. Not everyone is going to like or appreciate you. Oh well. There's not much you can do about that, so keep doing what you know is right. Keep showing up (see item #1 above), keep plugging away. It sounds simplistic, but it's the only way things are going to turn around. In essence, quit your crying and suck it up.

3. **Sports cliche #147 – "Worry only about the things you can control" – is real**: You hear athletes talk about this all the time. They say they can't concern themselves with the things they can't influence. Instead, all of their focus is on the items over which they have specific control: their attitude, their preparation, their game plan. It's the same for those of us who don't get paid to play a sport. In your career, in your personal life, in everything you do, there is a long list of things over which you exert control. Concentrate on those things. Don't worry about other people's attitudes. Don't worry about external circumstances you can't change. Don't concern yourself so much with the immutable things that simply are. Direct your time and attention instead to what could be.

4. **Have a plan**: Even if it only covers the next few years of your life, have a plan for what you want to achieve and how you're going to get there. Develop a vision for your life and what you want out of it. Otherwise, your existence will be a series of randomly connected activities with no real end goal in mind. You'll get somewhere, to be sure, but probably not where you want to be. Just set aside some time every once in a while to think about the future, both short term and long. You'll be glad you did.

5. **Be grateful**: You have so much in your life. You have a family

who loves you more than you can understand (though you will someday understand if you have kids of your own). You have a roof over your head, a car to drive, food to eat. Lots and lots and lots of people in this world lack one or more of those things. You were born with a silver spoon in your mouth, whether or not you recognize it. If you spend your time lamenting the things you don't have, you will be one unhappy individual. I'm telling you, you don't want to be that guy.

Happy graduation day, buddy. Enjoy every minute of it, because you've earned it.

I was Daddy. Now I am Dad.

This photo was on the front of the t-shirt I wore when I appeared on "The Price Is Right" in 2007.

March 13, 2021: When I launched my first blog in 2011, it was named "They Call Me Daddy."

After I took a hiatus and re-launched it, it became "They Still Call Me Daddy."

Then, a few years ago, I went with the more self-descriptive "5 Kids, 1 Wife."

What I only just recently noticed, though, is that the blog's meta tag search description still reflected the old names. Some of my posts on Facebook included this short description of the blog: "A father of five's account of life as a husband, PR professional, and of course, a daddy."

The part about "daddy" doesn't really make sense anymore since the blog's title has changed, so I edited the description simply to say "and of course, a dad."

It also doesn't make sense because I no longer have anyone calling me Daddy.

To all of my children, I'm just "Dad."

Well, Jared calls us "Scott" and "Terry," but that's only because he's sarcastically funny like me.

The last one to call me Daddy was Jack, who logically enough is our youngest. I think he stopped using that moniker once he turned 9 or so.

When I hear "Dad," I think of my own dad. Because that's what I called him.

He called me "Bear." Or "Slug." I don't know that he ever really explained the origin of either name. That was just what he called me, and I never thought anything of it. You can literally count on one hand the number of times in my life I ever heard him refer to me as "Scott."

Anyway, the Daddy-to-Dad and Mommy-to-Mom transition is an unheralded milestone in the parenting journey. Maybe it's unheralded because no one wants to admit their kids are growing up so fast or that they themselves are getting older.

I'm OK with it, I guess. I often miss the "Daddy" days, but not the associated diaper changes and spilled drink clean-up that went with them.

All things considered, this dad is good with being just "Dad."

My early approach to parenting depended heavily on Barney and Pooh Bear videos

September 19, 2021: Back when I worked nights and took care of Elissa all day, I had a go-to set of VHS tapes I would unashamedly use to distract her while I got stuff done.

This particular parenting technique is almost as old as television itself. You give the kid some Cheerios and a freshly filled sippy cup, sit them down in front of the TV, and let them happily watch something fun and age-appropriate while you fold laundry or whatever.

We had a wide range of videos we would show toddler Elissa, but the ones in heaviest rotation were undoubtedly Barney and Winnie the Pooh.

I know a lot of parents turn their noses up at Barney because they think they and their kids are too cool for a goofy purple dinosaur. To some extent I get it. Still, that goofy purple dinosaur did a whole lot to reinforce the lessons we were already teaching our child about kindness, politeness and putting the needs of others on par with or above your own.

God forbid, huh?

As for Pooh Bear, those videos were hilarious. There was a lot of adult humor in there that would make me laugh whenever I was able to pay some attention to the TV. Tigger alone is always worth the price of admission.

There were times I would feel guilty for pawning my parental responsibilities off on the VCR, but in retrospect, it was fine. There are certain things that must get done around the house, and sometimes you need electronic assistance in getting them done while simultaneously keeping your kid from wandering off and, say, tumbling down the basement steps.

Ultimately, all of our kids turned out OK. Maybe a tad neurotic like Pooh Bear himself, but really, who among us isn't?

RELATIONSHIPS & FAMILY LIFE

The unending chaos of marriage and children has several upsides, not the least of which is that it makes for great blog material.

1986: Mr. Cool takes his girl out on the town

Each time I look at this picture, I remember how much I miss that Chevette. And how much I regret wearing those shorts.

March 1, 2012: Twenty-six years ago tonight, my wife and I went on our first date.

I know this because I am the designated person in our relationship whose job it is to remember dates, anniversaries and the like.

My short-term memory is slipping year by year, but March 1st, 1986, will be forever seared into my brain.

For a long time, I thought Feb. 27th was our dating "anniversary." But then a couple of years ago I looked at a calendar from 1986 and was surprised to find the 27th was actually a Thursday. It made sense when I thought about it, though. I asked Terry out on a Thursday afternoon, and it was on Saturday the 1st we actually had the date.

The "ask" was the hardest part of the whole thing. Terry was a junior, while I was but a lowly sophomore. She was — and forever will be — eight months older than me, but we were both in band, which for whatever reason is a place where age differences tend to matter less than they do elsewhere in the high school ethos.

Being a football player, I was only in concert and jazz bands, not marching band, where a lot of band relationships were born. As fate would have it, though, Terry and I both spent our second-period study hall that year hanging out in the band room. Somehow (who knows how these things work?) we started noticing each other.

We talked a lot during those study halls, and she seemed to laugh at my jokes. (She doesn't really bother doing that anymore … we both know the only one who thinks I'm the least bit funny is me, so why pretend?) Any idiot could see we were rapidly falling in "like."

I wasn't just any idiot, though. I was the idiot actually involved in this thing, and I was scared to death to ask her out. Oh my goodness, she was so pretty. I mean like make-my-heart-race-and-my-stomach-flip-flop pretty. She still is.

It took a wise and mature senior, Connie Meier, to play matchmaker for us. I think Connie got tired of us skirting the issue and just decided enough was enough and that SOMEONE had to prod this moron into asking Terry out. So when I asked Connie if I had a shot, she said something to the effect of, "Uh, yeah, dude. Don't be so dense. Ask her."

That was about as much encouragement as I was going to get, so the only thing to do was to pop the question. Now if you've ever been in high school and have gone through this, you know you don't just *ask* someone to go out. You have to set it up. You have to figure out all the angles. You have to determine the right time and place. And most of all, you have to be Mr. Cool.

In retrospect, I find all of this hilarious. I already had it on pretty good authority that Terry was with the program here. No fancy prep necessary, really. I was, however, far too stupid to see this. I took a couple more days to figure out how and when I should execute my plan.

It helped that our lockers were right near each other. It was the last period of the day on Thursday. I was in Mr. Robertson's history class. I knew I would see Terry when I went back to my locker, so I decided this would be it. This was where I would make my stand, for good or bad.

As I walked back to my locker after the final bell rang, I had that dry throat, sweaty palms thing going. Why was I nervous? Connie told me this would work. What I jerk I am, I thought. This can't be that hard.

I get to my locker. Terry is standing at hers. Oh my gosh, she's so pretty. No way I can do this right now. Seriously, no way. But oh man, she's just beautiful. Look at her! And she's not dating anyone! And she likes you, you big dummy! Just do it! JUST DO IT!

ME: "Hey, Ter." (This is what I've called her for the last quarter of a century: "Ter," rhymes with "air." I'm pretty sure that's what I called her at that moment. At least that's how I remember it. I'll have to ask her if she remembers it the same. In any case, while I tried to do it in my casual Mr. Cool voice, I'm sure I was squeaking like the frightened 16-year-old I was.)

HER: "Yeah?"

ME: "You wanna go out tomorrow night?"

HER: "Oh! Uh, no, I can't."

OH NO OH NO OH NO OH NO!! SHE'S GOING TO SAY NO! FULL EMBARRASSED PANIC MODE! RUN AWAY! RUN AWAY!

HER AGAIN (quickly, probably seeing my look of alarm): "I have a youth group meeting at church tomorrow night. I can do it Saturday!"

ME (intense relief, trying without success to slip back into Mr. Cool mode): "Oh! OK, great. We can see a movie or something."

HER: "OK, we can do that."

And then I don't remember a thing for two days. I remember being on Cloud Nine. I remember being happy, relieved and nervous for the actual date. On Saturday, I picked her up in my styling yellow 1979 Chevrolet Chevette. Nothing, I mean nothing, says "Chick Magnet" like a yellow 'Vette!

It was a snowy might. I took her to the Mentor Mall, where we saw "Down and Out in Beverly Hills" with Nick Nolte and Bette Midler. Then we drove to Willoughby and I treated her to a gourmet dinner at the only place I could afford: McDonald's. Then I took her home.

As I drove down her street, I couldn't remember which house was hers. They were all made of brick, and at the time they all looked alike to me. I was cruising along at full speed when she suddenly said, "Stop, that's my house!"

So I hit the brake and immediately began skidding across the snow-covered pavement. The car turned 90 degrees to the right and came to a stop right in front of her house — actually facing her house, as it turned out.

Terry's house had a good-sized front window. Standing in that window at the exact moment my car swerved crazily, as God is my witness, was Terry's father. I could have died.

I sheepishly backed up and pulled into her driveway. I walked her to the side door. I told her I had a good time. She said the same. Mr. Cool leaned in for a goodnight kiss. And I kid you not, just as our lips were about to meet, I burped. I NEVER burp. Seriously, I'm almost incapable of doing it. I burp maybe 5 or 10 times a year. The God of the universe, who has never lacked a sense of humor, found that exact moment to be the time when I should take a step toward meeting my sparse Annual Burp Quota.

I was mortified, of course. I think we both laughed. But then we kissed anyway. And it was wonderful. I'm telling you, it was something. I will never forget it. I wish I could tell you at that moment I was thinking, "OK, this is the person I'm going to marry," but I don't think I was nearly sharp enough to know that. I just knew this beautiful girl had gone out with me. Had had a good time with me. And had kissed me. Whatever is 50 feet higher than Cloud Nine was where I spent the rest of the night. I went home a happy young man in that yellow Chevette.

As it turned out, we would be engaged in less than three years and married a few years after that. Kids would come one after the other for a 12-year period starting in the mid-90s. And it has all been amazing. I can't imagine I would ever change a thing.

Except the burping part. If I could go back, I would do everything humanly possible to hold in that burp. But other than that? Paradise.

Family movie night: Popcorn and trauma

March 28, 2012: Once every month or two, we try to have a Family Movie Night. Years ago when the kids were younger, this was a relatively easy thing to pull off. Now? Not so much.

You would think getting the family together to watch a movie would be a relatively easy process. And it should be. But there are two main obstacles to making it happen:

SCHEDULES: Living in our house are seven people ranging in age from 6 to 43, each of whom needs a social secretary. I cannot begin to keep track of the kids and where they are at any given time, nor can Terry, which is scary. If *she* gets confused by it, there's no hope for me. I'll come home from work on a Friday evening and will ask, for example, where Chloe is. It's not uncommon for my wife to respond with something like this: "I don't know. She's either at Miranda's, at Rachel's, at Chris Dorazio's, at track practice, at soccer practice, at play practice, at the movies, at the mall, at her piano lesson, at the zoo, at the park, or in Venezuela." All of these things are equally probable, and I'm sure Chloe told Terry where she was going before she left the house, but poor Terry can only retain so much information. Sometimes the location of her 15-year-old daughter gets pushed out of her brain.

RELATIONSHIPS & FAMILY LIFE

MOVIE SELECTION: Even if we manage to corral everyone into the living room for a two-hour block of time, we're still faced with the dilemma of finding a movie that will appeal to kids ages 6, 11, 13, 15, and 18, as well as their 40-something parents and whatever combination of boyfriends and/or schoolmates happen to be visiting at the time. Inevitably, a few of us end up compromising our individual tastes for the good of the group. But that's only after 45 minutes of intense negotiation rivaled solely by Middle East peace talks for passionate opinion and violent argument.

Eventually we settle on something, pop it into the Blu-Ray player and sit down for an enjoyable night together.

HAHAHAHAHA! You know I'm kidding. This never actually happens, or at least it doesn't happen quite that easily. Once we get everyone into the house and the movie selected, there's still the process of preparing refreshments. Forty-seven bags of microwave popcorn must be popped. Drinks must be poured into cups with lids so they won't spill onto our sectional couch (the one nice thing we own) or onto the floor, which would actually be OK because they would blend well with the Kool-Aid stains that have been there since a Family Movie Night in 2004.

Even more troublesome is that while the food and drink are being prepared, some of the denizens of the house take this as a sign that it's OK to start wandering away and/or engaging in various other activities. When we all finally take our places and prepare to press "play" on the remote, we do a quick count and realize someone isn't there. Annoyed, everyone starts screaming for that person to GET IN HERE NOW, rather than actually getting up and finding them. When the person does return to the living room, they are met with icy stares. I'm telling you, this is a tough group.

Speaking of people taking their places, this is another crucial element of the Family Movie Night experience. The sectional couch is big, but it's not going to hold everyone if we have visitors. Someone is going to have to sit on the floor, and no one really wants to. So the arguments begin over who's going to sit where, and why he keeps hogging the blanket, and how come she always gets the part of the couch that reclines, and I finally lose it and tell everyone to just SHUT UP SHUT UP SHUT UP SHUT UP!!! SIT DOWN AND WATCH THE MOVIE! QUIT YOUR ARGUING! WE'RE HERE TO HAVE A FUN MOVIE NIGHT AND WE'RE ALL GOING TO HAVE FUN OR I SWEAR I WILL BREAK YOUR NECKS! SO SHUT UP!

Capital letters don't do justice to my fury at these moments. Daddy doesn't lose it very often, but when he does, an uneasy peace will usually settle over the room. Those left without spots on the couch resign themselves to two hours on the floor. The others munch their popcorn silently. The movie begins. Ten minutes later, we forget there was ever any yelling and screaming, because we're all finally having fun as intended.

Except when someone talks during the movie and the others respond with a forceful "SHHHHHH!" Those moments can be a little awkward, but again, hurt feelings heal within minutes and we're back to enjoying ourselves.

Or at least I am. I'm smart enough to stake an early claim to the nice reclining chair. No way I'm sitting for two hours on that floor.

Mr. Please-Don't-Fix-It

April 3, 2012: I make no secret of my lack of mechanical ability. Nor do I think it would be possible to hide it anyway. Anyone who has seen me with a screwdriver knows I am to household repairs what William Shatner is to singing.

My wife will happily share this fact with anyone who asks. Her favorite story is undoubtedly The Cat Door Story.

This happened almost 20 years ago, back when we were first married. We had three or four cats, and their food/water bowls and litter boxes were kept downstairs in the basement. This required that the door to the basement always be left slightly ajar, which was often annoying.

Enter Manly Repair Guy (me). My perfectly logical thought was that, if we installed a little cat flap into the basement door, the cats could go in and out as they pleased and we could keep the door closed most of the time.

So I took a trip to a home improvement store. I can't even remember which one it was, but I'm sure it was one of those Home Depot/Lowe's Come-and-Embarrass-Yourself chain stores. I bought a cat door kit and brought it home, anxious to tackle this seemingly innocuous home maintenance project.

I took the door off the hinges (NOTE: The word "hinges" is an important plot point here. You'll see why in a moment.) and lugged it to the small workbench in the basement. We had a couple of different saws down there, so I picked one — almost certainly the wrong one, I'm sure — and managed to rip out a facsimile of a square hole that approximated the dimensions of the one shown in the directions.

My cutting wasn't straight, of course, and even when the metal frame was placed around the hole, some of the opening still protruded beyond the outside of the frame. Still, it wasn't that bad, and I managed to screw the frame into the door in what was undoubtedly a sturdy and somewhat-correct manner. Then I placed the rubber flap into the frame and voila...a new cat door, and one that was achieved without any blood loss on my part. I was triumphant!

I picked up the door and carried it back up the stairs to hang again. I turned it so that the hinges were on the correct side and... well, the only word that comes to mind here is "disaster." Because you see, when the door was positioned such that the hinges were where they were supposed to be, my newly mounted cat flap was in fact about six feet in the air at the TOP of the door, rather than a few inches off the ground where it was supposed to be.

Yes, I had cut the hole on the wrong end of the door. And as you might imagine, it's somewhat difficult to patch a hole that's 10 inches square. "Mortified" is how I would describe my state of mind at the moment I realized this huge mistake.

The only thing I could think to do at that point was to hang the door up and prepare to tell Terry when she got home from work. I don't remember her exact reaction when she walked into the living room and saw that the cat door was much closer to the ceiling than it was to the floor, but I seem to recall extreme laughter resulting in tears. This, to her, was easily The Greatest Thing That Had Ever Happened in the History of the Universe.

The jokes that followed were predictable, including speculation that we would have to buy the cats stilts in order for them to get through their awesome new door.

Luckily, Terry has the mechanical gene and was able to fix the

RELATIONSHIPS & FAMILY LIFE

problem for me. She drilled new hinge holes into the door so it could be hung the other way. Eventually the flap was at cat's-eye level where it belonged, but the story itself would not die. It will never die. My guy friends at church, virtually all of whom have the ability to build multi-story office towers with their bare hands, will bring it up at least once a year. They laugh and laugh about it, and it forces me to admit it IS pretty funny.

I am always happy to offer myself up as unskilled labor for anyone's home projects, but it comes with the warning that you should NOT give me tools of any kind. I'll haul, stack, rip out and handle your basic manual-labor chores and you'll be fine ... just as long as you keep, say, the chainsaw away from me.

As you might suspect, I don't do cat doors, either.

What people in my family actually mean when they say certain things

April 15, 2013

**When my kids say, "There's nothing to eat in the house,"
what they mean is…** "Of course I know there are things to eat in
the house. But they all require actual time and effort to prepare,
and I'm stunningly lazy. I need you to fix me something to eat
immediately while I sit and stare off into space."

When my wife says, "You're so weird," what she means is …
"You're a fool. I knew this when I married you, of course, but I
never really thought it would be this … *bad*."

**When my son is getting yelled at for something and asks,
"Why are you freaking out?" what he means is …** "I know what
I did was wrong and that I'm clueless. But I'm going to try and
save face here by turning the tables and making it seem like you're
doing something wrong. This has never actually worked to date,
but I'm going to keep trying."

**When my youngest child says, "I didn't do it" what he means
is …** "Well, yeah, I did do it."

**When my children are asked if they have homework and they
say, "No," what they mean is …** "Yes. Yes, I do have homework.
But I'm going to wait and do it tomorrow in homeroom instead of
doing the smart thing, which would be to finish it now while I have

RELATIONSHIPS & FAMILY LIFE

time. Instead, I'm going to watch this episode of 'Pretty Little Liars' that I've already seen. That sounds like a pretty solid decision."

When my 19-year-old daughter is asked if she spent the money she's supposed to be saving for college on concert tickets (again) and says, "Yep, I did," what she means is ... "Yep, I did." (Elissa doesn't beat around the bush. She pretty much tells it like it is.)

When my son is told he needs to get off the Xbox in 10 minutes because we're all going to watch a movie, and he says "OK, I will," what he means is ... "Nope, I won't. Amazingly, you keep believing me when I say I'll get off the Xbox at a certain time. Then, when I don't do it, you act like this is the first time it ever happened. As long as there are no consequences to this action, as repeatedly appears to be the case, I'm going to keep doing it."

When my wife says, "Someone needs to pick up Chloe from track practice," what she means is ... "YOU need to pick up Chloe from track practice."

When my wife says, "Someone needs to go to the store and get me some pizza sauce," what she means is ... "YOU need to go to the store and get me some pizza sauce."

When my wife says, "Someone should clean up the cat puke in the living room," what she means is ... "I could theoretically clean up the cat puke, but I know if I keep saying it enough times, eventually you'll clean it up yourself because, for some strange reason, it makes you feel guilty. You're such a sucker."

Did I ever tell you about the time my wife dumped me? Twice?

She cast me aside despite this nice pumpkin we carved together in 1987.

July 10, 2013: I have been in love with the same woman for 27 years.

I often say this is one of my greatest accomplishments, but I don't know that you could classify it as an accomplishment.

RELATIONSHIPS & FAMILY LIFE

"Accomplishment," to me, signifies conscious effort. I didn't make a conscious effort to fall in love with Terry. It just sort of happened when I was 16 years old. And it has lasted ever since. So I'm not sure you can say that being in love with someone is an "accomplishment."

Now, staying together with them? Nurturing that relationship? Strengthening your bond? *Those* take effort. *Those* are accomplishments. But being in love? I don't think I had much to do with that. That was God's work, and He did a very nice job of it, if I may say so.

Terry and I met when I was a sophomore in high school. She was stunningly pretty. I was passable in the looks department. To the point that you could take me out in public and not be overly embarrassed to be seen with me.

After less than a year of dating, I knew I loved her. Looking back, I was right about that.

You don't often know what love really is when you're 16 or 17 years old, but for whatever reason, I did. What I felt for her then was as genuine as what I feel for her now.

But it almost fell apart. Twice, actually.

Terry dumped me two times during high school. Once was between my junior and senior year in the summer of 1987. I don't remember much about that particular break-up, other than that it mercifully didn't last very long.

The second time was the following summer after I had graduated. I think it only lasted three weeks or so, but I'm not kidding when I say they were the worst three weeks of my life.

I was such a lost soul. I honestly couldn't fathom how I was supposed to go on without her. I just kind of existed. I hadn't yet started college, nor did I have a job at the time. So I existed. Miserably.

My mom remembers. She remembers me staying up late at night listening to sad music and just laying in my bed. Occasionally

I would call Terry. Most of the time she would tell me I had to stop calling her.

At one point she told me I needed to find someone else to be with, that it would be good for me. So I gave it a try. I went out a few times with a very pretty and smart girl.

But Terry (this is my favorite part of the story) didn't like that. I started my job at The News-Herald during our break-up period, and one night I came out of work to find a rose and a nice card from her tucked under the windshield wipers of my 1979 Chevy Chevette.

I drove straight to Terry's house. We got back together for good that night.

A few months later, when we were both 19, we got engaged. Less than four years after that, we were married. To the extent that I had anything to do with making this beautiful relationship last, I guess *that* is one of my greatest accomplishments.

But I realized the other night there's a potential dark side to all of this. Well, not a "dark" side, really, but there is a risk.

I have put everything into being with this woman. Everything I am is wrapped up in her. If something were to happen to her, I would be a lost soul again.

Knowing that is scary. I don't want to go back to that horrible feeling, though I just might have to. One day, anyway.

The reality of our collective situation as humans is that we have an expiration date. Whatever we build in this life simply ain't going to last forever, and that includes romantic bonds cemented by red roses left on Chevy Chevettes.

An extremely selfish part of me hopes I'm the one to die first, if only so I don't have to go through that dark time again. I have biology on my side, since women on average live longer than men.

Still, there's nothing to be gained by having these morbid thoughts, so I try to shut them out.

RELATIONSHIPS & FAMILY LIFE

Some nights just before I fall asleep, I turn my head toward her side of the bed and try to make out her face in the darkness. Often I can. Sometimes I can't.

No matter, though. I can always see her in my mind.

When I picture her, it can be as current mom-of-five Terry, when-we-just-got-married Terry, or occasionally 16-year-old Terry.

Every one of them is beautiful.

Then, and only then, do I drift off to sleep, content in the knowledge that whatever else may eventually happen, the girl I loved in 1986 is still laying next to me.

Twenty-seven years of that is worth just about any price, to tell you the truth.

These, believe it or not, are your finest days

Always lean into the chaos.

July 26, 2013: If you don't mind, I'd like for you to read a quote I've lifted from a novel called "Water for Elephants." It sets the stage for my ramblings, and you may find it as inspirational as I do:

> *Those were the salad days, the halcyon years! The sleepless nights, the wailing babies; the days the interior of*

the house looked like it had been hit by a hurricane; the times I had five kids, a chimpanzee, and a wife in bed with fever. Even when the fourth glass of milk got spilled in a single night, or the shrill screeching threatened to split my skull, or when I was bailing out some son or other ... from a minor predicament at the police station, they were good years, grand years.

But it all zipped by. One minute Marlena and I were in it up to our eyeballs, and next thing we knew the kids were borrowing the car and fleeing the coop for college. And now, here I am. In my nineties and all alone.

You don't have to have children to appreciate the truth of those two paragraphs. You need only be someone who has been through great stress at one point or another. Which is to say, all of us.

I have often waxed forlorn over the chaos that is my life. I find myself running hither and yon from dawn to dusk, and I'm not even sure where "yon" is, or why I'm supposed to run there.

Yet in all my complaining, never does it escape me that I love this life. I absolutely love it. While there are many people I admire greatly, I would not trade my existence for anyone's.

I constantly worry about my children. I constantly complain about their inability to clean up a mess. I constantly fret over the ways in which I fall short as a husband and father.

And it's wonderful. Every minute of it.

At the risk of sounding melodramatic, I think there's a certain nobility in what we as human beings do every day in support of ourselves and those we love. We sacrifice our time and energy for goals we like to believe are bigger than us, and we are better creatures for having done so.

Occasionally I find myself longing for the days when the kids are grown and things finally slow down. Yet I know for certain I'll miss this rat race.

So lately I've reveled in the bedlam. And so should you.

Whether you recognize it or not, my friend, these are your finest days. Embrace them. Learn from them. Grow in them.

These are the times that will define who you were. If you're playing your cards right, you should be pretty pleased with the outcome.

The 40-Year-Old Nephew

*Mark on the left, me on the right.
Sometime in the late 1970s.*

April 8, 2015: Today my nephew Mark turns 40 years old. When something like this happens, you are forced to deal with the fact that you yourself are not quite as young as you like to think you are.

I remember when Mark was born, sort of. I was 5 years old, hadn't yet started kindergarten, and spent most of my days in the kind of haze that is the domain of accident victims and 5-year-old boys.

I had some vague idea that another human being was about to become part of our lives, and that my brother Mark was apparently going to be this person's dad, but that's about it. Mark Sr. was only 17 years old at the time and still pretty much seemed like a kid to me (as I'm sure he did to himself).

So when Mark Jr. was born, it didn't take long for him to seem more like a little brother to me than a nephew. When you're 5 years old, you shouldn't have anyone calling you "Uncle."

Mark spent a lot of time at our house when he was growing up, which was generally OK but got a lot better when he became a teenager and was more fun to be around. In the few years I was working at a newspaper during college, I would sometimes come home from my job around midnight, and Mark and I would go out for a late-night meal at Denny's.

Occasionally I would let him drive my high-powered, chick-attracting 1979 Chevy Chevette, which was technically a violation of the law given that he wasn't yet of legal driving age, but turned out OK in the sense that he didn't actually kill anyone. This was 2 o'clock in the morning, remember, so the streets were pretty empty (I wasn't so stupid as to let him drive in rush hour or anything.)

Then I got married and started having kids, and I saw less and less of my little brother/nephew. We still see each other on holidays and we still laugh about the same stupid things, which makes 1990 seem not such a long time ago.

Now "little" Mark is married with a daughter of his own, and like I said, he's 40 years old today. All of which blows my mind and makes me wonder how my mom feels as her "baby" (me) creeps closer and closer to 50.

That's the whole Lion King circle-of-life thing, I guess. We get older. It happens. We grow up. It happens. We stop driving Chevy Chevettes. Thankfully, it happens.

So at the risk of making this occasion about me (yeah, I know, too late), let me just say happy birthday to Mark, my nephew, substitute little bro, fellow Sting fan, and long-time Denny's connoisseur. Here's hoping you get at least 40 more.

And here's hoping you're still around when your little daughter turns 40 so you can feel as old as I do right now.

Someone you love dies once, but you miss them forever

My sister Judi and my mom. I think about them a lot.

February 17, 2016: I feel compelled to say something today about my sister Judi. She would have turned 63 years old yesterday had she not passed away on May 12, 2009.

That's what happens when someone you love very much dies. You remember the date. It sticks with you. You will never be entirely happy on that day ever again.

Yesterday wasn't all that easy, either. I think of Judi a lot, but more so on her birthday, she and my brother-in-law Jess' wedding anniversary, every May 12th, etc.

It's interesting to me that people still post on Judi's Facebook page, usually on one of the above dates. It's not weird or creepy or anything; as a matter of fact, I think it's beautiful. It's a nice tribute to one of the nicest people you would ever in your life like to meet.

More than anything, I think it's therapeutic. When someone to whom you're very close passes away, the one thing you want is a chance to see them again. Tell them things you should have told them as a matter of course when they were still around. Just 5 minutes. That's all you ask for, just a few minutes to wrap things up, I guess.

In Judi's case, we didn't get that. Her death was sudden, shocking and life-altering. Just so tough on everyone involved, from Jess to her daughter Jessica to my mom.

Oh, my poor mom. As she said at the time, no parent should ever have to experience the death of a child, but she did. And she's still going strong at 83 years old. God bless her.

I'm not sure I have much of a point to make today, other than to acknowledge that I used to have a sister named Judi and now she's gone. Life goes on, but it's not the same.

Marrying young ... however you define "young" nowadays

April 18, 2021: On this day 70 years ago (April 18, 1951), my parents got married.

Mom had just turned 19 a week earlier, while Dad was all of 21. At the time, it was not unusual to be married at those ages.

Fast forward 41 years to June 6, 1992. That was the day Terry and I were married. She was 23 and I was 22. I had just graduated from college a few weeks earlier.

Again, while we were probably younger than most people becoming husband and wife back then, it's not like we were inordinately young for the early 1990s.

According to the U.S. Census Bureau, the average age for a first marriage in 2020 was 28.1 for women and 30.5 for men. What's more, less than 30% of Americans ages 18–34 are now married, vs. nearly 60% as recently as 1978.

Clearly, young people in this country are not in a rush to put a ring on it. At least not any time soon.

I'm not saying this is good or bad. It just is.

By the time Terry and I tied the knot, we had been together for more than six years. I had decided long before that she was The One, and she had clearly decided that, for all the warning signs of what lay ahead for her, she was willing to tie her fortunes to me.

Tennant-Ross

Terry Lynn Ross married Scott Patrick Tennant June 6 at Church of the Blessed Hope in Chester Township. The Rev. Alan Curtis officiated.

The bride is the daughter of Mr. and Mrs. Thomas A. Ross, 30004 Robert St., Wickliffe. The bridegroom is the son of Mr. and Mrs. Robert L. Tennant, 1807 Harding Drive, Wickliffe.

Christine Brooks of Colorado Springs, Col., was her sister's matron of honor with bridesmaids, Marianne Kuhar and Denise Palsa, both of Wickliffe, Brenda Jonath of Huntsburg and Tammy McGranahan of Middlefield, both cousins of the bride, and Cathleen Ross of Mentor, sister-in-law of the bride. Katie Burnette of Wickliffe, Gina and Leah Sabruno, both of Willoughby, all cousins of the bride, and Jessica Veneri of Euclid, niece of the bridegroom, were flower girls.

Mark Tennant of Wickliffe served his brother as best man. Ushers were Kevin Buchheit of Euclid, Mark Tennant Jr. of Willowick, nephew of the bridegroom, Nathan Woods of Wickliffe, Bob Brooks of Colorado Springs, brother-in-law of the bride, and David Ross of Mentor, brother of the bride.

Mr. and Mrs. Scott Tennant

A reception at the Italian American Club in Wickliffe honored the couple before a wedding trip to Walt Disney World and Cocoa Beach, Fla. They live in Wickliffe.

The bride is a 1987 graduate of Wickliffe High School and is a payroll clerk for Lincoln Electric in Euclid. Her husband is a 1988 graduate of Wickliffe High and a 1992 graduate of John Carroll University in University Heights. He is a sportswriter for The News-Herald.

It's not like we met when we were 20 and got married a year or two later, which was common in our parents' generation. We knew each other well and were great friends in addition to being a couple.

As we approach our 29th anniversary, I would say it worked out for us. I know others our age with similar stories.

All of which is to say that whatever the demographic trends are, being "too young" to marry is a subjective thing. I got engaged when I was barely 19 and had people tell me that was nuts and we should wait a bit. I knew they were wrong.

Others are clearly not ready to enter into a long-term commitment when they actually do, and more often than not, those unions end in divorce.

Maybe it's good that people are waiting until they're more financially and emotionally stable before taking the plunge nowadays. All I know is, I was basically a kid when I got married and it's still the best decision of my life.

Your results may vary.

He was my friend

Possibly the best picture Fred ever took

February 22, 2022: Last night we lost our cat Fred. He had been very sick and was scheduled to be put to sleep this afternoon, but he decided to go on his own.

This is not especially remarkable, I know. It happens thousands of times every day in homes, veterinarians' offices and animal shelters around the world. We're certainly not the first people to go through it.

RELATIONSHIPS & FAMILY LIFE

But that doesn't make it any easier. There's nothing mundane or routine about losing someone who has been part of your life for a long time, whether they're human, feline, canine, rodent, bird, etc.

Fred and his brother George have been members of our family for 14½ years. We got them from the animal shelter in 2007. Terry and I went out that day saying we were going to get a single female cat, and instead we came home with these two snow white goofballs.

At some point, and I really can't say when it was, Fred decided I was his human. He got along with everyone in the house – every human anyway ... I don't think he ever really liked another cat besides George – but for whatever reason, he loved me most.

For years, Fred would jump into bed at night and lay right up against me. He was gone every morning when I woke up, but most of the time when I was falling asleep, he was right there.

When I had Lyme Disease in 2012 and was laid up for the better part of a couple of weeks, he spent most of his time in bed with me.

He would purr (loudly) for anyone willing to pet him, but he always seemed to find an extra degree of volume for me.

In some ways, Fred lived his life in perpetual angst. A lot of that had to do with the other cats who came into our home after him (Charlie, Ginny and Molly, along with the now-departed Bert). But he had his brother, with whom he often snuggled in the winter months for warmth. Together, Fred and George got through everything life threw at them.

There were a few times over the years when we thought we had lost Fred, including once less than a year into his time with us when he was sick and we were going to put him down. Then Terry discovered a wad of dental floss wrapped so far around the back of his tongue that the vet had completely missed it.

Suffice it to say, he went through all nine of his lives and probably a few more.

95

He started to develop urinary tract issues over the past couple of years, and it got to the point that he had to sleep in the basement storage room at night because he couldn't be trusted not to pee in random places.

A few times he peed blood, and each time the vet would give us a course of antibiotics.

The blood would eventually clear up, but I'm not sure the medicine had anything to do with it.

We had it all but confirmed yesterday that Fred had some sort of cancer. Could be bladder, could be kidney, who knows? He had so much fluid in his abdomen that it was difficult to see his organs on x-ray, which we're told is a pretty good indicator of cancer in a cat.

In the last couple of weeks, he had been lethargic and not eating, and the bloody urine had come back in full force. He was miserable, and there's no doubt it was his time.

Putting him down would have been the right thing had he not beaten us to the punch. Because even when it's hard, that's what you do for your friend.

To those who don't have pets or who have never been especially close to an animal, it probably sounds silly to talk about a cat as your "friend." After all, apart from his very expressive meows, I did most of the talking in our relationship. There wasn't a lot of dialogue there.

Yet somehow I think there was. I loved him and he loved me, and that was pretty much all that needed to be said or understood.

You know the day will come when a pet will be gone, but you're never quite ready.

I wasn't even sure how to say goodbye. I think he already knew I was a big fan of his, but I told him so anyway, just to make sure.

A proper sendoff is the least I could give the poor guy. After all, he was my friend.

OTHER THINGS ON MY MIND

I am more than just a husband and a father,
though admittedly not much more.

What your choice of board game says about you

December 28, 2011: We're a board game kind of family.

And by "board game," I don't just mean the ones where you roll a dice and move a little piece around a sheet of pressed cardboard, though Lord knows we have plenty of those. I also mean checkers, chess, cribbage, Scrabble, Yahtzee and oodles and oodles of card games.

In our downstairs storage room is a seven-foot cabinet filled top to bottom with almost every game you can imagine. We never lack for choices.

One reason we like board games is because we like winning. If there's one thing I've passed down to my kids, it's a competitive streak. I like to win. They like to win. There is little mercy expected and almost none shown during one of our family board game sessions.

You might say, "But isn't it about having fun?" And we would respond, "Yes, but isn't the greatest fun seeing an opponent land on Boardwalk and Park Place when you own them with hotels, and watching the other person reluctantly hand over the small fortune in Monopoly money they've spent two hours accumulating?"

We like to play virtually anything, but there's a subtle message conveyed in the specific board game you select. Like the car you drive or the clothes you wear, a board game says something about you. Here's what I'm talking about:

CLUE People who like to play Clue are violent sociopaths. They have no interest in free-market real estate (Monopoly), choosing a career and raising a family (Life) or out-and-out lying (Balderdash). They want a game that involves the gruesome bludgeoning or stabbing death of a rich guy, and the subsequent trial, conviction and execution of the murderer (who, by the way, always seems to be Colonel Mustard when I play). Be careful, though. If you beat them at Clue, they're liable to reenact the murder scene with you playing the part of Mr. Boddy.

BATTLESHIP Battleship is a game of luck. Winning is random, unless you're playing a young child who packs their ships into that little "I have no idea what I'm doing" square of doom. I'm not saying that being a good Battleship player is the equivalent of being a good slot machine player, but....well, yes, actually I am saying that. They're both hit and miss. But hey, there's no shame in the fact that you lack deductive reasoning or any other socially redeemable skills.

MONOPOLY Like Monopoly? Then you're probably a cheater. Yes, you heard me, you're very likely a cheater. No honest person genuinely enjoys Monopoly, because an honestly played game of Monopoly takes 14 hours. The game only ends in a reasonable amount of time if the banker is giving himself interest-free loans on the sly, or if someone else steals a deed to complete a monopoly ("Wait, you have Marvin Gardens? I don't remember you buying that." "Oh yeah, it was an hour ago. You must not have noticed.") You might be saying, "Well, I never do either of those. I don't cheat at Monopoly." Yeah? Do you do that thing where you put money on Free Parking and give it to the next person who lands there? Then you're a cheater. It's not in the rules. Look it up.

TRIVIAL PURSUIT If Trivial Pursuit is your first choice, you're an insufferable, overly competitive know-it-all. I should know, because I'M an insufferable, overly competitive know-it-all, and Trivial Pursuit is always my first choice. Why? Because I know that no matter who you are, there's a good chance I'll destroy you. My mind is filled with useless knowledge. Rarely is it of much use unless I'm playing Trivial Pursuit or appearing on the occasional television game show. Never play Trivial Pursuit with someone who wants to play Trivial Pursuit, that's my advice to you.

CHESS, CHECKERS, SCRABBLE, BOGGLE, STRATEGO AND ANY OTHER OF THOSE GAMES AT WHICH I'M NOT VERY GOOD People who choose these games are smarter than me. I can do random trivia, sure, but that's no indication of intelligence. That's just having a good memory and the gift of instant recall. These are games of strategy that require clear thinking, a quick mind and the ability to anticipate your opponent's moves. I lack those skills, and the people who have them are exactly what I want to be when I grow up. But let me get them on the other side of a Candyland board and I'll wipe the floor with them. I have five kids, man. I'll be past Queen Frostine and on my way to victory before they even know what hit them.

Put me in, Coach (or at least give me a brownie)

We were probably talking about the post-game snack.

March 19, 2012: For more than a decade, I have been a volunteer youth sports coach. This is an important position in which parents and kids alike rely on you to teach valuable lessons of teamwork, discipline and sportsmanship.

I'm kidding, of course. What parents and young athletes care most about can be summarized as follows:

PARENTS: Winning, their child's playing time and the soaring cost of youth sports participation

KIDS: Snack

I can understand the parents' priorities, because in addition to being a coach, I'm also the parent of young athletes. But I've never been able to explain the kids' fascination with their post-game or post-practice snack.

This is especially true with my U8 soccer team. These are kids in kindergarten, first and second grades. My halftime instructional/pep talks usually go something like this:

ME: "OK, guys, gather around me! Good job in the first half! We did a lot of good things and I really like how you guys hustled out there. Just a couple of problems, though. Let's watch our passing, and let's make sure we keep good spacing between us and our teammates, OK? Any questions? Yes, Johnny?"

JOHNNY: "Who brought snack?"

ME (taken aback even though I've been asked this question 8 bajillion times during my coaching career): "Snack? Um, I don't know. I'll have to check the list."

At this point, one of the other kids raises his/her hand and volunteers that his/her mom is, in fact, the one who brought snack today. This is followed by a barrage of excited questions from the other kids: What did your mom bring? Is there enough for us to have seconds? Did she bring those little packets of Oreos, too? And on and on and on … I quickly move to restore order:

ME: "Hey, hey, hey! Guys! Pay attention! Listen, we'll all get snack after the game is over. But right now we have another half of soccer to play and we need to work on our defense." (Johnny raises his hand again. I eye him warily before acknowledging his presence.) "Yes? Johnny?"

JOHNNY: "How come Mackenzie's mom forgot to bring snack last week? I was really sad that I didn't get any snack."

MACKENZIE (clearly offended by this attack on her mother): "She just forgot, OK? Don't YOU ever forget anything? She felt really bad that she forgot to bring snack. She said something about having all these darned kids and not being able to remember which one is supposed to be where at what time, and that my stupid soccer coach keeps signing her up for snack when she has no time to go out and buy anything because she's a single mom and works three jobs. And then she cried. She does that a lot. Anyway, I'm telling her you said that!"

ME (again attempting to restore order): "GUYS! GUYS! GUYS! Can we not talk about snack now? Anyone who mentions snack again before the end of the game won't get any snack at all, do you hear me? Now let's get back out onto the field and have some fun!"

JOHNNY (to himself): "I just really wanted snack, is all."

What I've learned over the years is that when kids show up for, say, a soccer practice or game, the last thing they want to do that day is play soccer. They would rather be on the playground. Or trying another sport. Or looking at dandelions. Or standing on their head. *Anything* except playing soccer.

Therefore, you have to keep things moving and interesting. Instead of boring drills, we engage in a variety of games and activities that are tangentially related to the sport of soccer but surreptitiously teach them the necessary foot skills. We move from one to another in rapid-fire fashion, because no matter how well-behaved the kids generally are (and they really are good kids, every one of them), the minute they put those shin guards on, they all suddenly have the attention span of Corky from "Life Goes On."

The parents are good people, too. Understandably, they want their child to derive the highest possible benefit from the soccer or baseball experience, and they can be touchy if they perceive the slightest injustice in the amount of playing time allotted to the little tyke. Many of them firmly believe their 7-year-old has the talent to earn a Division I college athletic scholarship and that you as the volunteer coach are the only thing standing in the way.

Still, parents are integral to the world of youth sports, fulfilling a variety of useful functions.

The most important of which, of course, is bringing snack.

Five songs that make dads of daughters start blubbering

Melanie and me on our way to a 50s-themed Daddy-Daughter Dance, 2008

(This post is far, far, far and away the most widely read thing I have ever written. Most of my posts garner 200 to 300 page views. Last I checked, this one had more than 27,000. It's a subject that resonates with people, and one that apparently ranks pretty high in certain Google searches.)

April 6, 2012: Inside every father of a daughter is a big softie. No matter how hard and tough the guy may seem, I guarantee he has a tender place in his heart for that little girl.

The music industry knows this and has, on more than one occasion, taken advantage of it by producing songs designed solely to make us cry.

There are relatively few things that make me cry. If a Cleveland sports team ever wins a championship, I will cry. *(NOTE: This was written pre-2016, remember. True to form, I did tear up a little when the Cavs and Monsters won titles that year.)* This is silly, I know, but I won't deny it.

I mist up at most Hallmark movies, too, though I usually blame it on dust in the room or something.

Anything sentimental to do with my kids will also make me cry. I'm no different than most other dads in this respect.

So here, then, is one man's list of the Top Five Daddy-Daughter Songs Designed to Make Grown Men Weep. We'll go in reverse order:

#5 – "Daddy's Little Girl" – The Mills Brothers No list of this kind would be complete without the most requested Father-Daughter Dance song of all time. From the very first verse, The Mills Brothers go for the heartstrings: "You're the end of the rainbow / My pot of gold / You're daddy's little girl / To have and to hold." If any of my daughters make me dance to this song at their wedding, I will collapse into a sobbing heap right then and there. That's it, just four lines into the song and I'll be done. I'll telling them this now so they can be prepared for major embarrassment on their big day.

#4 – "Stealing Cinderella" – Chuck Wicks Country singers are experts at exploiting the daddy-daughter relationship. We could actually have filled this list with nothing but country tunes. For my money, this one is the best. It tells the story of a guy going to his girlfriend's father to ask for her hand in marriage. It's obvious the dad worships his daughter, and that "to him I'm just some fella riding in and stealing Cinderella." Note the Cinderella figure will play a major role in a just a moment …

#3 – "When She Loved Me" – Sarah McLachlan Perhaps a surprise entry. On the surface, this isn't necessarily a daddy-daughter song. It's from the "Toy Story 2" soundtrack, and it's sung from the perspective of a doll whose owner has grown up and doesn't play with her anymore. But the song has always reminded me of my daughters, and sometimes specifically of Elissa and the two years or so when I worked nights and was with her every day while Terry was at work. "Through the summer and the fall / We had each other, that was all / Just she and I together / Like it was meant to be." Excuse me for a second, someone must have emptied the vacuum cleaner bag because it's getting really dusty in here.

#2 – "Butterfly Kisses" – Bob Carlisle Darn you, Bob Carlisle. You're an evil, evil man. This song is terrible, and by that I mean it's awesome. What makes it terrible is that it's one of those "let's follow the little girl as she grows up and becomes a woman and end on her wedding day as her father walks her down the aisle" songs. Which of course makes you realize that time passes impossibly fast and that you're probably not making the most of it. Every time I hear this song, I go looking for Melanie to see if she wants to play a board game or go outside or just do anything except grow up like her rotten sisters.

#1 – "Cinderella" – Steven Curtis Chapman "'Cause all too soon the clock will strike midnight and she'll be gone." Oh boy. The next time any of the kids asks me to play with them, I don't care what I'm doing at the moment. I will drop it in a heartbeat just to get in one more game of Junior Monopoly or watch one final video before they grow up and move on. The clock strikes midnight awfully, awfully fast.

Psychoanalysis through band instruments

Pulling the family band together (even with a few extra, non-family members) is always a treat.

April 20, 2012: We all play musical instruments in our house (except Jack, but give him a few years). It's what we do.

It started 30-plus years ago when Terry and I began playing the flute and saxophone, respectively. In fact, it was in the high school band room that we met. Music has been a big thing for us since the start of our relationship.

Then along came the kids and, one by one, they've been picking up instruments. Even little Jack can bang out some tunes on the piano, and he plays a mean game of Wii Music.

I've always thought a person's choice of instrument says something about them. Like flutists tend to be quiet and shy, while tubists are loud and brash. I've seen too many exceptions to that rule over the years to put a lot of stock in it, but I choose to continue believing it for two reasons:

- It's much easier to believe stuff you want to believe, rather than paying attention to facts.

- On a related note, it's much easier to blog about stuff you want to believe than the stuff you have observed to be true.

In that vein, let me offer this little psychological profile of the people in my family based solely upon the instruments they play:

TERRY

Instrument: Flute

What It Says About Her: Flutists (we would also have accepted "flautists") want to play music but don't want to draw too much attention to themselves. This is Terry. She is certainly no spotlight-seeker, but she does enjoy the opportunity to play her flute when it presents herself. She is, to me, the quintessential flute player.

What Instrument She Should Have Played: Actually, the flute fits her to a tee. But if I had to pick another instrument for Terry, it would be the clarinet. Clarinetists are a lot like flute players. (Interestingly, Terry herself often wishes she had played the trumpet.)

ME

Instrument: Saxophone

What It Says About Me: Sax players all secretly want to be guitar players or rock drummers. When faced with the choice of picking a band instrument, if they can't bring themselves to play the drums, they go with the coolest, most rock-sounding instrument they can think of. Of course, this analysis used to hold a lot of weight back when there were actually sax solos in pop songs. There hasn't been a decent, original saxophone solo in a Top 40 song since, I would guess, 1989.

What Instrument I Should Have Played: Bassoon, apparently. One time I performed at solo and ensemble contest, and that's actually what the judge wrote on my evaluation sheet: "You should be playing the bassoon." I had no idea how to take that remark.

ELISSA

Instrument: Oboe

What It Says About Her: Few oboists actually start out as oboists. Most start on the clarinet or another instrument and somehow find their way to the oboe a few years later. Elissa is an exception. She started directly on the oboe, a notoriously difficult instrument to play, in 4th grade. This might suggest she loves challenges and always picks the most difficult road. In Elissa's case, though, I think it was more her crazy dad convincing her to play an out-of-the-way instrument just so, eight years later, she could get a college scholarship. I feel bad about this in retrospect.

What Instrument She Should Have Played: The triangle. Seriously, Elissa would rock the triangle like no other, um, trianglist has in history.

CHLOE

Instrument: Baritone horn

What It Says About Her: When the kids first start band, they attend a Meet the Instrument Night where they can explore each instrument up close and personal, and even try to make a sound out of it. I accompanied Chloe to this event, where once again I pushed for a less-popular instrument with the thought of a college scholarship or at least being a section of the band unto herself. Chloe is a person unto herself. She's unique. The choice of a big, low brass instrument just confirms that.

What Instrument She Should Have Played: Trumpet. No doubt about it, there's a trumpet player inside of Chloe. I should have pushed her in that direction. The trumpet is a featured instrument that often carries the melody. Chloe would have loved that. And she CAN actually play her sister's trumpet, not surprisingly. She also plays piano, harmonica, and probably the lute, for all I know.

JARED

Instrument: Saxophone

What It Says About Him: See the analysis of Jared's father above.

What Instrument He Should Have Played: Something for tall people. The kid is 6 feet tall in seventh grade. String bass, maybe?

MELANIE

Instrument: Trumpet

What It Says About Her: This is where the theory really breaks down. I tend to think of trumpet players as loud, flashy people. That's not Melanie. She's a relatively quiet, beautiful person (not that trumpet players aren't generally beautiful). Maybe she uses the trumpet to project or amplify her true self. As I've said before, being the fourth of five kids ain't an easy job, folks. The fact that Mel does so well in life is darn impressive to me. That she took up the trumpet and can actually play the thing is even more remarkable. I can't get a sound out of it.

What She Should Have Played: I would have bet large amounts of cash that Melanie would play the flute like her mother. Short of that, I can see her as a violinist. Quiet, gorgeous and necessary.

JACK

What He Says He Wants to Play When He Gets Older: Drums

My Reaction to That: Oh, good Lord, no...*(NOTE: It turns out Jack eventually went with the trumpet, and he is great at it.)*

Our new thousand-dollar dishwasher

May 23, 2012: We bought a new dishwasher.

I realize how unimportant this is to you, but I'm thrilled about it. I end up being the one who loads the dishwasher most nights, so this is one appliance that matters to me.

The old dishwasher cost something like $400. It lasted four years. The new dishwasher was about $1,000. Can I assume it's going to last a decade? Probably not. But I'll tell you what, it had better hold up longer than four years.

We bought the dishwasher at B&B Appliance, one of those family-owned stores that has been in business since the Stone Age. I'll bet these people were selling hand-crank washing machines and wooden TVs in the Oklahoma Territory 150 years ago. They may not always have the best price, but their service is excellent and they stand behind their products.

I know this mostly because my father-in-law Tom shops there. Tom is not a guy who just rushes into things like buying thousand-dollar dishwashers. He has many years of experience in buying (and fixing) appliances, so if he says B&B is good, I'm with him.

The guy who sold us the dishwasher is named Flint Parker. Really, that's his name: Flint Parker. Isn't that great? If I'm being honest, I'll admit part of the reason Flint was able to close the deal with us was because of his name. Plus, he looks like Morgan Freeman, and I like Morgan Freeman.

Another reason we bought this particular dishwasher is because it's a KitchenAid. Some years ago I bought my wife a KitchenAid mixer. The thing not only weighs five tons, I think it could mix concrete. Terry only uses it to make cakes and stuff, though, so I can't confirm the concrete thing. But it's definitely heavy duty and will last a long time. I'm hoping the same is true for the dishwasher.

Yet another reason we bought it is because it has four spray arms across the bottom. Most dishwashers (including our old one) have only two. Flint walked around the store opening up various dishwashers and showing us that, unlike the KitchenAid, every one had only two and occasionally three spray arms.

I asked why four spray arms is better than two, and Flint looked at me like I was slow. I guess I understand, but if four spray arms are so revolutionary, why don't other manufacturers make their dishwashers that way? I didn't ask Flint because I was afraid he wouldn't like me, and I'm not sure I could handle having Morgan Freeman not like me.

Flint has been working at B&B for 26 years and selling appliances for 50. That means he's at least in his late 60s, but he didn't seem that old to me. He was wearing a button-up sweater vest and looked good in it. Not many people look good in a button-up sweater vest, let me tell you. I guess it takes someone with the confidence of a veteran appliance salesman to really pull off that look.

Anyway, we went ahead and bought the dishwasher, which now that I think about it didn't really cost a thousand bucks. The total was a thousand with delivery and installation, and I was happy to pay extra to have it brought to my house and hooked up. I suppose I could manage the job myself after much reading of the instruction manual and the requisite weeping and gnashing of teeth. Really, though, it was worth the extra cash to come home and see it correctly installed and ready to use.

It's really quiet. And it has buttons on top of the door instead of on the outside. It feels very space age to me, like the sort of dishwasher you would see on Star Trek. If I had the money, I would equip our house with nothing but Star Trek appliances. That's a very tempting thing to do, especially when you walk into a store with all the latest models.

Believe me, B&B had all the latest models. Washing machines, dryers, TVs, ovens, refrigerators. They were all there, and they were all insanely expensive. They had a model kitchen that Terry very much wanted. I did some quick math in my head and calculated that all of the appliances together in the model kitchen would set you back about 25 grand. That's some serious cash ... cash we didn't have.

So for now we'll content ourselves with the new dishwasher. And with the fact that we now have a friend named Flint Parker. He was nice enough to give us his email address. I think I'm going to email him and let him know how quiet his four-armed KitchenAid dishwasher is.

One soldier's life, long forgotten

May 28, 2012: Every Memorial Day, I think of Merwin Brewer.

There probably aren't many people who think of Merwin Brewer on Memorial Day anymore, or on any other day, for that matter. He has been dead for nearly a century.

Merwin Brewer was an American soldier who died on the Western Front at the tail end of World War I. His official address was listed as Cleveland, Ohio, but he was born in my hometown of Wickliffe, Ohio. Our local American Legion post is partially named after him (Brewer-Tarasco).

The annual Memorial Day parade is a big deal here in Wickliffe. It's one of the better parades around, with two marching bands, lots of candy and 45 minutes or so of entertainment for anyone willing to stand and watch the whole thing.

Every year, the American Legion has a group of local kids walk in the parade carrying signs with the names of Wickliffe natives who have died in war. And every year at the front of this group is a young person holding a sign emblazoned with Merwin Brewer's name.

The 30 seconds or so it takes for that sign to pass by is the only time the Memorial Day parade turns truly somber for me. This is partly because I have a morbid fascination with the First World

War and the way millions of young men were killed during it. No war is good, but this one was particularly tragic.

Merwin Brewer died on November 13, 1918, from wounds sustained in combat. That was two days after the war officially ended. No one wants to be the last man killed in a war that's already over, but Merwin was one of those who fell just short of making it through alive.

Merwin served in the Argonne and in Flanders, both the scenes of brutal, bloody fighting. I often wonder exactly how he died. Probably from a shrapnel wound. Artillery was the #1 killer in the war, and countless soldiers succumbed to infections and internal injuries suffered when they were hit by flying hunks of metal from exploding artillery shells.

His story doesn't sound particularly distinctive. His life ended the same way millions of others ended, probably in some military hospital. But Merwin Brewer is as real to me as any one of my family and friends, because he was born in the same place I was born. He was a real person whose death, now long forgotten, probably brought unimaginable grief and sorrow to his family back in Ohio.

And he was only 22 years old. Just a baby. "Virgins with rifles," that's what Sting called the soldiers of the First World War.

I'm as guilty as anyone of treating Memorial Day as a festive day off from work instead of a time for reflection. But while I'm eating my grilled hamburger later today or lounging outside with my family, I promise I'll spend at least another couple of minutes thinking about Merwin Brewer.

It seems like the least I can do.

The story of my vasectomy you didn't ask for

January 25, 2016: I recognize you probably don't want to hear about my vasectomy, and if that's the case, you're free to stop reading right here.

But if, for whatever reason, you're OK moving forward with this subject, you can't say I didn't warn you.

It has been nearly 10 years since I underwent The Big Snip. I know this for two reasons: (a) I always remember weird dates, and (b) My youngest son, Jack, will turn 10 this Wednesday.

It was after Jack was born, you see, that Terry and I decided Tennant Offspring, Inc. needed to shut down operations. Or at least it needed to shut down the production of new offspring and instead focus on nurturing the ones it already had.

Right from the start I knew it would be much easier for me to undergo the sterilization process than it would be for her. Women's reproductive systems are complex, Rube Goldberg-like machines involving all sorts of parts that can only be accessed through major surgery.

Men, on the other hand, are wired fairly simply. Vasectomies are way easier to perform (and way easier on the patient) than hysterectomies. And after all, it only seemed fair for me to be the one on the table after Terry had courageously birthed five babies in the space of 12 years.

OTHER THINGS ON MY MIND

So vasectomy it was. I can't remember how or why I selected Dr. Schneider as the urologist to do the deed. At the time I don't think I realized he was 12 years old.

Or at least it *seemed* he was 12 years old. He was clearly younger than me, and he looked younger than the students at my kids' schools. But he had a fancy diploma on the wall and appeared to have all the required instruments in his office, so I went in assuming he knew what he was doing.

Which of course he did. One thing I learned during two years as managing editor of *Urology Times* magazine back in the late 90s (really) was that vasectomies are extremely routine procedures that urologists learn to perform early in their training. There's just not much to them.

From the patient's perspective, I can say there were only two things that disquieted me:

1. Laying on a table essentially naked while another man fiddled with my privates and talked about the Cleveland Browns

2. The use of what seemed to be a five-foot needle injected into An Extremely Sensitive Region in order to numb that region before Dr. Schneider made his incision

The needle was of course not five feet long, but the key point here wasn't so much its length as its sharpness. The only pain I experienced in the entire procedure was when that needle (WARNING: EXTREMELY GRAPHIC MEDICAL TERM ABOUT TO BE USED) pierced my scrotum and, from what I could tell, kept going up into my abdomen and stopped just a few inches shy of my neck.

That was ... unpleasant. Really unpleasant. But it only lasted a few seconds, and it didn't approach Baby Coming Out of Tiny Opening on the unpleasantness scale, so I was OK with it.

After that, the whole thing was actually kind of – and trust me when I tell you how hesitant I am to say this, but there's really no other word for it – nice. And by "nice" I mean that Dr. Schneider and I had a great conversation about sports while he went about his business. He, like me, is a big Cleveland sports fan, and we lamented how comically bad our teams are.

When it was over and he told me I could get up, I was kind of sad. Not because I was anxious to have him keep poking, cutting, cauterizing and generally rearranging my Man Parts, but because I really liked talking to him. I realized he probably had to get home and finish his homework, though, so I was OK with it.

When I got home myself, Terry looked at me anxiously and asked if I was feeling OK. And I was. The numbing agent was still in full effect, so I wasn't feeling anything.

Later I felt something. Not an intense pain or anything, but just an annoying, enduring ache. Which is when we broke out the bag of frozen peas. That's not just a cliche, folks, it really works. Sitting on that bag of peas watching TV was mostly what I did that night and much of the next day.

A few days later I tried to do my normal morning run and it just … well, it hurt, you know? The constant tugging of gravity on an area that had, less than 100 hours earlier, been subjected to scalpels and forceps and the like was unpleasant. Again, not Having a Baby Unpleasant, but still unpleasant.

After a week or two, the pain went away and I was right as rain. I had to go back another time to make sure the whole thing "took," if you know what I mean, but all in all, it was the very definition of a minor procedure.

The moral of the story, guys: It's not that big a deal. I know you WANT it to be a big deal so you can tell gruesome war stories, but disappointingly, the procedure is quick and easy, as is the recovery.

Just have those frozen peas at the ready. Seriously, you want to have those frozen peas.

An October roller coaster of emotions

(This was — and still is — a long post. Absurdly long. You don't have to read it. Really, you don't. I just had a lot to say at the time and I felt I should warn you.)

October 18, 2016: Bill Cosby began what is, for my money, one of his funniest stand-up comedy routines many years ago by saying, "I must tell you about my problems driving around San Francisco …"

Of course, there was nothing "must" about it. He *wanted* to tell you about those problems, and you wanted to listen because you knew it was going to be funny. Or at least you wanted to be nice to Bill, back when he seemed like a person to whom you should be nice.

In the same way, I must tell you about the emotionally exhausting ordeal that has been my October 2016 to this point. I don't "have" to tell you about it, but I want to tell you about it, and I thank you so much for listening. Or reading, I guess.

SPORTS, KIDS, AND PAINFUL NUT SHOTS

If you're someone who indulges me on Facebook, you know that most of my posts these days have something to do with my kids' sports activities. The youngest three are all in the latter stages of their soccer seasons, and of course Jared, my 18-year-old, is also serving as the kicker for my beloved Wickliffe Blue Devils football team.

There are highs and lows when you're the parent of an athlete. You rejoice when they succeed, you agonize when they fall a little short, and you cry inside when they have a difficult time or seem to be losing their enjoyment of the sport, for whatever reason.

Jack, who is 10, is playing his first season of travel soccer. He's a defender, and his team is very good. Very, very good, actually. Jack has had periods when he plays every minute of every game, and other times when he sits the bench. This level of soccer is new to him, and while he has mostly adapted well, there are still things for him to learn. His coach, Arturo, is tough but fair. You earn your spot and you work to keep it. That's the way life goes, and I don't think 10 years old is too early to learn the lesson.

Melanie is a sophomore in high school, and statistically she has had a tougher time this year than she did as a freshman. She's a forward, so Mel measures herself by statistical output: goals and assists. As of this writing she has one of each. Last season she had something like seven goals and two assists. The fact is, the talent level on her team has risen noticeably this year and playing time is harder to come by. Again, you get it by earning it.

Virtually no soccer player I've coached or watched over the past 15 years works harder than Melanie. She's the soccer equivalent of a hockey grinder — someone who goes out there and fights for loose balls, bangs bodies and plays physically when needed, and consistently puts her head down and does the dirty work in front of the goal. Those are the types of things that help teams win, even if they don't always show up on the stat sheet.

Mel is going through a crisis of faith these days. She's a bit disillusioned by her position in the team hierarchy, and she doesn't see much room for upward movement in the next two seasons. My advice to her is simple: Keep doing what you're doing. Work

OTHER THINGS ON MY MIND

on every facet of your game...ball control, first touches, decision making, speed conditioning, etc. Be the hardest working player on the field. The rest will take care of itself.

Not a bad lesson there, eh?

And then there's my boy Jared. He's one of two boys I have, of course, but for a long time before Jack came along, I simply referred to him as *The* Boy. And let me tell you, that boy is one busy dude.

He's a starting forward on the boys high school soccer team and the team's second-leading scorer. He does the kicking thing in football, and also straps on his saxophone and plays (while still in his football uniform) at halftime on Friday nights. Every day is another practice, game or rehearsal, or a combination of all three.

He is nearing the end of a football career that began three years ago, but more importantly, of a soccer career that started when he was a fuzzy-headed, six-year-old kindergartner. That's how it is when you're a senior in high school: You do something for years and years and work so hard to get better at it, and then suddenly it's over. Unless you're one of the handful of people who go on to play at the collegiate level, you're finished. Just like that.

This realization is coming quickly for Jared. It will all hit him in a few weeks when his fall activities end without the promise of a next year. Part of him will be relieved, I'm sure, as the grind of fall sports and band starts to wear noticeably after a while. But part of him will grieve, no doubt in that silent, I've-got-this, keep-it-to-yourself manner of Jared.

And if I'm being honest, I will grieve right along with him. I love watching him play. Just love it. I love watching all of my kids play, but you only get the Senior Experience once, and it has been wonderful. He plays some sort of key role in everything he does, and I couldn't be prouder of him.

But the rest of Jared's life is calling him, urging him to move on from where he is now and to experience new adventures. I'm excited for him, but I'm going to be so sad when this all comes to a screeching halt in November.

Oh, but you know what I won't miss? Jared taking hard-hit soccer balls to his testicles. Seriously, this happens to him at least once a season. He'll be going about his business playing the game when someone on the other team will launch a rocket shot that absolutely destroys his Man Region. Jared goes down, he gets tended to by a snickering coach or trainer, both teams on the field laugh while trying to seem like they're not, Jared gets up and hobbles off, and he comes back later in more or less decent shape.

Jared being escorted off the field by his coach after one of his "unfortunate" incidents

This has happened so many times I can't imagine watching him go through it again. Maybe it's just as well this soccer thing is about to end.

As for football? Well, Jared has settled into a nice routine every game of executing a series of pooch kickoffs and extra points. He had some trouble on the extra points earlier this season, but now he has rounded into form, and the team itself is 6-2 and on its way to its best record in 15+ years. There may even be playoff football in our future, which is exciting.

My son, the kicker

I start thinking about whether Jared will be called on to decide one of those playoff games. He hasn't kicked a single field goal in three years of varsity football. Not one. Twice he has lined up to attempt field goal kicks, and both times they were blocked.

What if they send him out there to decide a game with a 35-yard field goal in the final seconds of the fourth quarter? Physically I know he can do it (easily, actually), but mentally, how will he handle it? How will *I* handle it, for crying out loud?

I'll tell you how I'll handle it: by fainting. Seriously, I'll just pass out on the spot. I'll never see whether the kick is successful because I'll be laid out flat on the bleachers while everyone else is watching nervously.

I'm tough that way.

SAINT TERRY: THE SAVIOR OF OUR LIVES

I am married, it turns out, to one of the most amazing people on the planet. I've said this before, and if you know her then you know the truth of my words. She is a whirlwind of ability, empathy, laughter and grit. She keeps six of us going every day while maintaining a house that has somehow not fallen down around us in the 13 years we've lived there.

She is, in short, the most remarkable person I've ever met. By a long shot. No disrespect to you or me or anything, but we simply don't come close to her on the Awesomeness Scale.

Which is why her recent emotional struggles have come as a bit of a shock.

When I say "emotional struggles," I don't mean she's going nuts or anything. I just mean that even the mighty Terry has reached the limits of her endurance at a time of year when she is constantly being called on to drive a kid to practice, mend a band uniform, clean up a mess someone else has made or tend to a very sick cat (more on that in a bit).

Some people can handle more than others. Terry's threshold for work and responsibility is high, but it is not infinite. And over the past several weeks, we've finally crossed it.

Which is why I've been on the kids and on myself to step up our games. It never should have gotten to this point in the first place. The family, as a whole, allowed itself to grow entirely too dependent on Mom. That's not good for her, and it's certainly not good for them. You raise independent, resourceful adults by forcing them to be independent, resourceful kids.

We're working on it. Some are better than others, but I'm confident we'll all get there.

In the meantime, Mom has applied for a job for the first time in nearly 20 years. I won't get into the details here, but suffice it to say she has an interview in a few days and I know she'll do great. Because that's who she is. If and when she gets the position, even though it's only part time, we're all going to have to adjust and fend for ourselves a little bit more.

Which, by all accounts, is a good thing.

YEAH, HE WAS JUST A CAT, BUT...

A few hours ago, before I had the chance sit down and eat my lunch as I type out this post, I took our cat Bert to the vet and had him euthanized.

That's the medical term for it: "euthanized."

What it means, in reality, is that I allowed the doctor to inject a lethal substance into his veins that almost instantly ended the life of the beautiful mess that was Bert.

That phrase "beautiful mess" came from our friend Kelly Gabriel, and I love it. They are the two words that best encapsulate the Bert ethos.

My oldest daughter, Elissa, found Bert sick, cold and alone on Eddy Road one winter evening a few years ago. She called Terry, and they took this smelly, bedraggled creature home. A long bath, a warm bed and several bowls of cat food later, he joined our household as Cat #4 (there would later be five).

We don't know where Bert came from, but it was always clear that his ordeal left him permanently shy of 100% health. He was fat, he walked with a limping waddle, and one eye appeared to be semi-functional, at best. But he was so, so lovable. He enjoyed being petted. He enjoyed being fed. He enjoyed sleeping in sunbeams.

And best of all, he seemed to enjoy being part of our family.

Bert (right) napping with his best friend in the world, Ginny

Not long ago, it became clear something was wrong. First it was an infection in his mouth. Then he wasn't eating or drinking much. We quickly discovered he *couldn't* eat or drink much because something was wrong with his tongue. It stuck out sideways and he couldn't coordinate it with his mouth and jaw to draw in food and water.

There was something neurological going on with Bert, though we honestly never paid the vast sums it would have taken to determine exactly what. A brain tumor? A stroke? Something else? Who knows? What was obvious was that Saint Terry – who made it her personal mission to care for Bert every day despite the fact that he was unable to clean himself and quickly became repulsive and smelly – couldn't hand feed this increasingly emaciated feline every day for the rest of his life.

So we decided to put him down. I took him in because there was no way Terry should have had to do that herself. She had already done more than her fair share. The vet, Dr. Richman, was incredibly kind and empathetic. It was almost as if it pained him more to put Bert to sleep than it did for us to let it happen.

The process itself, if you haven't been through it, is quick and almost painless for the animal. Bert was gone before they even finished fully injecting him with whatever it is they use for that sort of thing. His eyes didn't close. They were just kind of half open. But the life that had been in them moments earlier was no longer there. It was his body, but it wasn't Bert.

I teared up a little, and not just for Bert. My heart hurts for him, but it hurts even more for the people in my house who loved him. They're dealing with this in different ways, so if you're a praying person, I would appreciate it if you said a few words for them this week.

I know that sounds silly to those who don't own pets. I realize he was "just a cat," but to say that is to deny the reality that Bert was also a presence in our house. He was a personality with whom all of us dealt, just as surely as we deal with each other every day.

And now he's gone. And he's never coming back. The dynamic in our home changes just a little. Among the remaining four cats, it changes a lot.

Ginny, our little semi-kitten, loved Bert. She slept practically on top of him, helped him clean himself, tagged along sometimes when he walked around the house, and clearly preferred spending time with him more than any of us. It was cute.

Then Bert got sick and Ginny's tune changed quickly. She avoided Bert. Even hissed at him. A few times in the last week or two, I would see her sneak up on Bert to sniff him. She would get close, take in a good whiff and quickly recoil.

You can't blame her. This was nature at work. Pure instinct. Bert had the smell of death about him, and animals avoid death. It's how they're programmed. What had been a loving relationship, at least the way we saw it, quickly became avoidance. Fickle little Ginny moved on to Charlie as her cat buddy. Together I'm sure they'll continue terrorizing the white cats, brothers Fred and George.

And they'll do it without the help of Bert. I don't know how cats' memories work, but I wonder if there will always be a little bit of him in Ginny's mind. I wonder if she'll miss him. Maybe not.

We sure will.

IN THE END, AN OCTOBER TO REMEMBER

In a few hours, my Cleveland Indians will play for the right to advance to the World Series for the first time since 1997.

The year 2016 has been a magical ride for those of us who call ourselves Cleveland sports fans. We endured a comically long period of athletic ineptitude in this town that ended abruptly in one 10-day stretch this past June when the Lake Erie Monsters won the American Hockey League's Calder Cup, and their Quicken Loans Arena roommates the Cleveland Cavaliers captured their first NBA title shortly thereafter.

I have seen so much losing in my lifetime you would think I would still be on Cloud Nine over these championships.

But in a very real way, I'm not.

And I'll be the first to admit the reason is silly and childish. I never fully embraced or celebrated either title because I wasn't here to see them. I was in Europe for both. When the Monsters won the Cup with a dramatic 1-0 Game 4 victory over Hershey, it was Terry and Jared who sat in our season ticket seats and rejoiced. I was in a hotel room in London on a business trip.

When the Cavs completed their incredible comeback series win over the Golden State Warriors a week later, I woke up to the news in Barcelona.

That wasn't how it was supposed to happen. It just wasn't. I was supposed to be there with Jared when the Monsters won, and I was supposed to be watching with Jared in our living room when the Cavs finished off the Warriors.

But I wasn't. Best laid plans and all that sort of thing, I suppose.

Again, I know this is stupid and that I really should be happy for Terry and Jared that they got to witness what they did. I just struggle with it. My dumb little cross to bear.

Terry and Jared pose with the Calder Cup, 2016

Enter the 2016 Cleveland Indians.

The Indians were the first sports team with which I fell in

love (a statement I realize makes almost no sense to someone who isn't a sports fan). Specifically, it was the 1979 Cleveland Indians. They were a mediocre team that won as much as they lost, finishing in their customary sixth place in the American League's East Division.

But they were my team. The first time I had ever had a "my team." I followed those guys every day in in the paper and on TV. Toby Harrah, Duane Kuiper, Andre Thornton, Bobby Bonds, Mike Hargrove, Wayne Garland. Names that mean almost nothing to most people now but that meant a lot to me as a 9-year-old fan.

The Tribe has been to the World Series twice in my lifetime, losing in 1995 to the Atlanta Braves and (painfully, unbelievably) in 1997 to the Florida Marlins.

And now they're almost back. One more win and they play for the title, preferably against the Chicago Cubs, because that sort of perennial loser vs. perennial loser story is too good for the journalist in me to pass up.

I've been staying up late to watch the Indians games with Jared and paying the price the next day in the form of bloodshot eyes and a stuffy nose. I need more rest, but I won't get it until the playoffs are finished.

Hopefully they end with the Indians celebrating yet another Cleveland sports championship. As the guy said on TNT the moment the Cavs won their title, "Cleveland is a city of champions once again!" Unreal.

I want the Indians to win because I want the Indians to win, of course. But selfishly again, I want them to win so I can jump up and down with Jared and hug him and think of my dad and probably start crying.

I cry easily these days. I cry thinking about people who are gone (my dad, my sister), pets we've loved, my kids, my sports teams, etc. Only some of those things are truly worthy of tears, but

OTHER THINGS ON MY MIND

there you have it.

I am, in the end, a nearly-47-year-old suburban father of five doing my best. And I realize my dad was much the same before me.

So it goes.

I just assume you're a good person (or "The time I gave $80 to a stranger named Maurice")

March 17, 2017: There are relatively few things I can say I strongly believe, but one is that most people have genuinely good intentions.

I truly believe this. I'm not saying most people are "good" (whatever that means) but that, by and large, they intend to do good.

There are exceptions of course, though I'm not adept at recognizing them. I have almost no ability to detect when someone is trying to take advantage of me. Call it naivete or whatever, I just don't pick up on it.

The result is that you could easily get me to buy a fake deed or give you money to help with some nonexistent problem. I choose to believe people don't do that to each other.

My wife, on the other hand, knows better. She can point to several examples in which she would say my faith in humanity ended up biting me in the proverbial backside.

The most shining example of this was Maurice. Maurice was a man I met at a Shell gas station a couple of years ago as I was pulling in to put some air in my tires. He flagged me down and explained that he and his girlfriend were staying at a nearby hotel, that they didn't have any money, that they had gotten into an argument (I

OTHER THINGS ON MY MIND

think … I can't remember the details now), and in a nutshell, that he needed money for food and transportation home.

You get the idea.

If you're like most people, you probably would have reacted in one of two ways:

Option A: You would have politely declined his request for money and driven away

Option B: You would have given him a few bucks and driven away

I, however, chose Option C, also known as The Dumb Option. I told Maurice to get into the car so that I could take him to Mr. Chicken for food, which I would pay for. I didn't know Maurice from Adam (or Eve, for that matter). If any of my kids ever took a total stranger into their car like that, I would freak out. But it seemed OK for me because Maurice was a nice guy.

NOTE: My wife recently pointed out that many of my dumbest decisions include the sentence "he really seemed like a nice guy." She's probably right.

Anyway, we chatted as we drove to Mr. Chicken, and I enjoyed the conversation. Maurice really WAS a nice guy, at least outwardly. When we got to the restaurant, I told him to order whatever he needed for him and his girlfriend. And there may have been a child involved, too, I can't remember. I think the order came to $20 or so.

Then, as we got into my car and started driving back to his hotel, Maurice said the only way he and the girlfriend could get home was by taking a cab. And since it was on the other side of Cleveland, it was going to be really expensive. I wasn't sure how much of his story I believed at this point – even I'm not a complete fool, though I know it seems like I am – but it was clear he was in need, so I told him I would take him to the bank and we would withdraw some money for him.

If you're a sensible person, you're probably staring at your screen slack-jawed at this point. "What the #^&?! were you thinking?" is something you likely want to say to me now. I know, I know. But did I mention how much of a nice guy he was?

I got $60 out of the cash machine and gave it to him. He had asked for more but I told him that was all I could spare. Then I drove him back to the spot where I had originally picked him up. He thanked me as he got out of the car and told me he would be in touch to pay me back, which I never believed. Because again, I may be stupid, but I'm not dumb. Mostly.

Wait, you're wondering, how would he be able to contact me? Because I gave him my cell number. "YOU WHAT?!? WHY DIDN'T YOU JUST SIGN OVER YOUR HOUSE TO THE GUY, YOU DUMB ****?"

I know, I know, in retrospect maybe not a good move. But I thought that was the end of it.

Until a week or two later when I was sitting on a hillside in West Virginia. (This is absolutely true.)

Terry and I were attending my mom's family reunion, which every year is held in a rural park on the West Virginia/Pennsylvania border. We had climbed up a grassy hill and were sitting there by ourselves talking when my phone rang. I saw it was a Wickliffe number and picked it up, figuring it was somebody I knew.

It WAS somebody I knew. It was my friend Maurice! He was at a different hotel this time and needed a place to stay, but at the moment he was short of cash and was hoping I could pay for his room until he was able to reimburse me.

It was only at that moment, I think, when I realized maybe not everyone is a completely honest person. In a few seconds, I would fall from the ranks of "completely honest" myself.

I wasn't about to pay for Maurice's hotel room, so I told him (truthfully) I was out of town and couldn't just come down and

OTHER THINGS ON MY MIND

bail him out. He said that was probably fine and asked if I could come to the hotel the next day when I was back. So I did the only thing I could think to do.

I lied through my teeth.

"Oh, I won't even be back in Wickliffe until Thursday," I told him. "And even then I have work and I'm going to be really busy."

We were going back to Ohio that same day, but I wasn't telling him that.

Then came one of those moments that lives on in my relationship with Terry. After I told Maurice I wouldn't be home until Thursday (it was Saturday), I covered up the phone and said in a loud whisper to Terry, "I'M LYING!"

She busted up. Of COURSE I was lying, and of COURSE she knew I was lying. There was no reason for me to tell her I was lying, but I felt the need anyway. To this day, any time Terry or I say something that obviously isn't true, one of us will look at the other and loudly whisper, "I'M LYING!" We have fun together.

Maurice hung up and, surprisingly, I never heard from him again. I really thought I would. Terry, from time to time, will mockingly ask me if he has called recently to arrange repayment of the $80 "loan" (which is how much it was when you add up the food and the cash). I tell her to shut up, she laughs at me, and life goes on. This is how you stay married for nearly 25 years.

Anyway, I recount all of this not to suggest that I'm some virtuous person, but to drive home two essential points:

1. Despite my stubborn belief in the inherent goodness of most people, I will concede there are indeed exceptions.

2. I'm an idiot.

You instinctively knew both of these things already.

Dear random number that texted me...

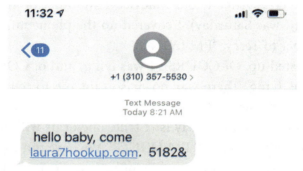

Screenshot of the mystery text in question

March 19, 2021: Thank you for the invitation, Laura! That is so very kind of you. Your wonderful words of greeting ("hello baby, come") immediately put me at ease and made me realize I had just made a new friend.

I would be happy to "hook up," as you call it, though I'm not sure what that means. I assume we will be doing the sorts of things friends do, like bowling, flying kites, crafting, book discussions ... that sort of thing.

I have to tell you, Laura – may I call you Laura? – your text made my day. It's not often someone from an unknown Los Angeles number texts you out of the blue with the intention of striking up a friendship, and I can only conclude you are a selfless and giving person.

One thing, though, Laura, and this is important: I have to ask my wife if it's OK for us to go out and do stuff together. I can't imagine she would say no (who would be against friends getting together?), but I've been married 29 years and I just feel like you should get permission from your wife before engaging in this "hooking up" thing.

Again, I'm not sure what it is, but I'm excited to find out!

Here's my thought: You fly here from L.A. on, say, a Friday. We'll take in a movie Friday night and grab dinner. Then you can sleep over our house and we'll have all day Saturday to do whatever we want. We have some great museums here in Cleveland, and I wouldn't want you to come to our fair city without a trip to the Rock and Roll Hall of Fame.

I'm sure Terry wouldn't mind cooking us dinner Saturday night, after which (assuming you have the energy for it) we'll be looking at three or four uninterrupted hours of board games. I know, I'm pumped about it, too! We have a whole closet full of them, though I must ask that we include Life and Pay Day on our list. You can choose the rest.

On Sunday morning we'll go to church, of course, then I can drive you back to the airport. Along the way we'll stop at our local public library where Terry occasionally works. It's a real gem and I would be so proud to show it off to you.

Of course, I'm riffing here and these are just ideas. You may have other things in mind for us to do, in which case please feel free to throw out suggestions.

I'll tell you, Laura, your text has really restored my faith in humanity. As a middle-aged man with a credit card and a stunning vulnerability to flattery, I cannot imagine anything going wrong here.

Write back soon!

The smell of pipe tobacco, four decades later

March 27, 2021: You know what they say about certain smells triggering the deepest memories? It's true, in my experience, and recently I was powerfully reminded of it.

I go out walking very early, which means I don't generally come across many people. I was walking around 5:30 in the morning the other day when the scent of burning pipe tobacco suddenly filled my head.

Someone nearby was clearly smoking a pipe. I surmised it was someone standing on the porch of one of the houses I was walking past, though it was still so dark I couldn't make out anyone.

No matter, though, as that smell instantly transported me back to a very specific time in the late 1970s. I would wake up on a Saturday morning and go into the kitchen, and almost inevitably my dad would be sitting at the table playing solitaire (the real kind, non-electronic) and smoking his pipe.

He kept the tobacco in a zip-up leather pouch. Sometimes I would open the pouch and take a big whiff because I loved the smell of it. It didn't smell quite as good when it burned, but it still wasn't nearly as unpleasant as the unavoidable stench of cigarettes that was seemingly everywhere back then.

I also associate a certain sound with that smell: the sound of

OTHER THINGS ON MY MIND

shuffling cards. Dad had a lot of experience playing cards, so he was a very good shuffler.

Shuffling cards and pipe smoke. That was the Saturday morning sensory soundtrack of my youth. For a few seconds as I walked, I was taken back to that time.

My dad has been gone more than 20 years, but as far as I was concerned, he was right there with me. It was 1978, and the only two things ahead of me that day were a morning of cartoons and an afternoon playing with friends.

In a moment I snapped back to reality and turned my attention to the World War I podcast to which I was listening. The rest of the walk was that much more pleasant, though

Heartfelt thanks to the person who was smoking that pipe. It's not a healthy habit, but I'll admit, you made my day.

My mom used to give me a dollar to go and buy a loaf of Italian bread at Fazio's. I got to keep 25 cents.

April 7, 2021: It was the early 1980s, I guess. When she was between shopping trips and the family needed bread, my mom would send me to the grocery store.

It was always Italian bread. Sliced with seeds from Fazio's, where she did most of our shopping. I have very little Italian blood in me, but that's virtually the only kind of bread we ever ate.

The store was, I don't know, maybe a 5-minute bike ride from home if I hurried? No more than 10 minutes, for sure.

Once I got there, I would enter, take a right and cut through one of the cashier lines, then another right followed by a left to get to the bakery. I would order the bread, which would be placed in a see-through plastic Fazio's bag and handed over to me.

I would take the bread, get into a 12-items-or-less line, and pay for it using the crisp dollar bill Mom had likely gotten from the bank when she cashed Dad's last paycheck. The bread cost 75 cents. That left me with a quarter, and that quarter never made it home.

I would always insert it into the video game stationed at the store entrance. The game changed a few times over the years, but the one with the longest tenure I can remember was Defender.

OTHER THINGS ON MY MIND

I loved Defender. I once wrote an article for a middle-school English class on how to succeed at the game. Mrs. Crow gave me an 'A' on it, God bless her.

I would stand there playing Defender for however long I could hold out before losing my allotted three ships. If I had done well enough (which occasionally happened), I would enter my initials into the game as one of the high scorers.

Then I would grab the bread, go outside, get back on my bike and ride home. The whole process rarely took more than 45 minutes.

I would pay a large sum of money for the chance to go back and do it once more.

It was a simpler time, you understand.

"Hi guy!" Did your hometown (like mine) have its own unique catchphrase?

April 16, 2021: Recently, my old classmate Bob Risko posted something on a Facebook group of which I'm a member called "You know you're from Wickliffe if …"

Wickliffe is, of course, the city where I've lived my entire life. I'm sure there are plenty of these types of FB groups where people who grew up together share memories and experiences common to their particular town.

Bob's post, completing the sentence "You know you're from Wickliffe if …" simply said: "… you have used the words 'Hi guy.'"

99.99999% of the world would look at that post and rightly ask, "Huh?"

The other .00001% of us grew up in the 1970s and 80s in Wickliffe, Ohio, and those words made us all smile.

"Hi guy!" was just something we said to each other. In my time, it was in response to someone who said or did something stupid or weird. Some of the comments under Bob's post suggested that, in the years before my time, it was used as more of a noun (someone could be a "hi guy") and was considered more of a direct insult.

It was fascinating to read those comments. Many Wickliffe-ites who hadn't uttered the words "Hi guy!" in decades were suddenly waxing nostalgic about them.

OTHER THINGS ON MY MIND

What intrigues me about this phrase was that it was entirely a Wickliffe thing. We never met anyone from a surrounding city who said it.

Conversely, it wasn't just a small, isolated group of Wickliffe kids who used it. It was clear from the comments that it sprang up in the 70s and was used through the 80s and into at least the early 90s.

And now it's dead. No current Wickliffe kid has any idea what "Hi guy!" is all about.

One of the big revelations in this discussion came from Terry Jo DeBaltzo, who revealed the origins of "Hi guy!" It was a phrase used in TV commercials for Right Guard antiperspirant in the early and mid-70s.

So here we have a peculiar little phrase that someone took from a TV commercial and began using. It gained greatly in popularity only within one particular city, evolved in meaning over time, and died away two decades after it sprang up.

You could have lived your entire childhood and teen years in a neighboring city like Willowick or Euclid without ever hearing the words "Hi guy!" Whereas it was a regular part of the vocabulary of the similarly aged Wickliffe kid whose house was maybe 100 yards away from yours just across the city line.

I am no linguist, but I find this fascinating.

Oh, and also, hi guy!

Why I never took another shop class after 8th grade

May 18, 2021: The obvious answer to the headline is because I'm one of the least handy people you will ever meet. I can fix computers but almost nothing mechanical. I can perform basic car maintenance, but anything electrical or plumbing-related baffles me. I don't even paint well.

But there's another reason I never took what we referred to as "industrial arts" classes beyond 8th grade, and it involves one of the most interesting characters of my middle school years, Mr. Lowell Grimm.

Mr. Grimm was my shop teacher, my football and basketball coach, and a 50s music aficionado. He was intense, though as I understand it, by the time I had him in the early to mid-1980s, he was a less-intense version of what he had been when my brother had him as a teacher in the very early 70s.

I did see him break at least two clipboards over Ron Vargo's head, though. Ron was, thankfully, wearing a football helmet each time, but still.

He yelled at us quite a bit, but that was fine because a lot of teachers and coaches yelled at us then. You were just kind of used to it.

I also think he liked me, though he could never figure me out. In football, for example, I was a running back who ran much more effectively to the left side of the line than the right. He noticed

OTHER THINGS ON MY MIND

this and once said to me, "Tennant, you're an enigma."

He often called me "Lou," since I would wear my dad's "Lou's Tire Mart" softball shirt over my shoulder pads at football practice.

Anyway, we had to produce a relatively complex mechanical drawing as our end-of-year final exam in Mr. Grimm's 8th-grade industrial arts class. I was not a good draftsman, nor would I ever be. But I gave it a shot.

I took the finished drawing up to Mr. Grimm's desk and handed it to him. It was, at best, maybe C-level work.

Mr. Grimm looked at the drawing, then he looked up at me. He looked back at the drawing, then he looked at me again.

"Tennant," he said, "I'll tell you what. If I give you an 'A' on this, do you promise never to take another industrial arts class again in your life?"

I didn't plan on any taking any more shop classes anyway, and I knew I didn't deserve an "A" on the drawing, so I jumped on this deal immediately.

We both kept our end of the bargain. Mr. Grimm gave me that "A," and I never set foot in another shop class again, assuming you don't count Mr. Lewis' electronics class the following year in 9th grade (which I don't).

Mr. Grimm, incidentally, was shot during the terrible Wickliffe Middle School shooting of 1994. He was trying to save kids at the time, of course, because for all his intensity, he really did care about us.

I interviewed him some years later for the Wickliffe Schools Alumni Association newsletter and he talked about the shooting, how he survived it and his recovery. Not surprisingly, he said going through something like that tends to mellow you out, both as a teacher and as a person.

I think he was a big softie at heart all along, though, and I have the "A" on my final 1983-84 report card to prove it.

When I was a freshman in high school, the seniors seemed like adults to me

June 9, 2021: My high school housed grades 9 through 12, which meant that, at the beginning of every school year, you had 14-year-olds barely starting puberty sharing the building with nearly 18-year-olds who looked like they dropped their kids off at daycare that morning before coming to class.

When I was one of those 14-year-old freshmen, I idolized the seniors in the Class of 1985. To me, they looked, talked and acted like adults.

Names from that class that come immediately to mind include Vince Federico, Lisa Strmac and Kevin Horten, among many others. These were grown-ups to me, and it always made me feel that much smaller, younger and more immature.

In retrospect, this is silly. I look back now and realize these people were essentially just slightly older children. At the time, though, the difference in age, experience and demeanor seemed huge.

When I played football, there was a tradition in which, at one practice a year, the freshman team offense would go up against the varsity defense, and vice-versa. This was full-go, full-contact football, and I always assumed the intention was to allow

OTHER THINGS ON MY MIND

ninth-graders the chance to experience what getting hit by a varsity player felt like.

I was on that freshmen offense as a running back, which meant I was fair game for these 12th-grade adults to maul as they pleased. I took a handoff and ran right into Vince Federico, a linebacker with the ability to break full-size cars in two with his bare hands.

Vince smashed me to the ground, but then he popped up, offered his hand, pulled me to my feet and said something like, "Good job, big boy."

I will never forget that. The hit stung for a moment, but his encouraging words stayed with me.

Which makes me wish that, by the time I was a senior, I had taken the whole job of being a leader and role model more seriously.

I was captain of the track team, for instance. I worked hard and like to think I set a good example that way, but I wish I had interacted more directly with the underclassmen to help them improve. I wasn't mature enough at that point to do it, to my own loss.

There is probably a lesson there for all of us as parents, aunts/uncles, managers, business professionals, etc. Someone is almost always looking to you to set the right tone or to model correct behavior, whether you realize it or not.

Bottom line: Be Vince Federico and not me.

Here's why I was on the local TV news in 1977 (and never really saw it)

October 7, 2021: One day in 1976, I walked into our living room and announced I was bored.

My dad, knowing the kinds of things that interested nearly-seven-year-old me, suggested I write a letter to a famous person like the President.

I was intrigued by this idea, but I did him one better (or thought I did): Rather than writing to President Ford, I would write to Gov. Jimmy Carter, who was running for the presidency against Ford.

I don't remember what I wrote, but whatever it was, I'm sure it was done in pencil on one of the yellow legal pads I kept in my room. (You may wonder why a six-year-old had yellow legal pads. I do, too. It was a long time ago.)

Anyway, I remember getting some sort of form letter response a month later from Gov. Carter, who went on to win the election by a fairly narrow margin.

That was enough for me. I thought it was pretty cool.

But then, in early January of '77, a large envelope showed up at our house. I think it came via registered mail. It was an invitation to President-Elect Carter's inauguration in Washington, D.C.

At the time I don't think I understood the significance of this. All I knew is we weren't going to attend.

I don't remember why this decision was made, but I think it had something to do with the fact that we would have had to supply our own transportation and would have been small faces in a crowd of many thousands.

There may also have been something to the fact that both my parents were Republicans, and they wouldn't necessarily have been thrilled to go and celebrate the inauguration of a Democratic president.

Whatever the reason, I don't remember being too put out.

Fast forward a couple of weeks later to mid-January. I'm in gym class at Mapledale Elementary School, where I'm a first-grader. A local TV news crew shows up and talks to my gym teacher. Then they start walking in my direction.

It turns out they're there to film me. I am incredibly confused by this, though the on-air reporter, legendary Cleveland television newsman Neil Zurcher, explains it's because I received a personal invitation to the presidential inauguration.

They get me on camera doing some rudimentary tumbling, as we were in the midst of a gymnastics unit. Then we go to our classroom, where I sit at my desk and they interview me. I don't remember any of the questions or any of my answers.

They tell me it's going to air as part of the 6 o'clock news on WJW Channel 8, which is exciting.

At some point that day it started snowing. And it kept on snowing. All day. Lots of snow. A real blizzard (almost exactly one year before the epic Cleveland Blizzard of 1978). As a result, all planned stories for that 6 o'clock newscast are shunted aside in favor of weather-related coverage.

Somehow we find out my piece will probably air during the 11 p.m. news later that evening. I think my sister Judi was the one who called the station to get this update (as I recall, she was also the one who called them about me in the first place).

At that time of my life, I went to bed every night at 9 p.m., almost without exception. I rarely stayed up until 11.

I remember laying down that evening on the couch, intending to stay awake until the news came on. But I don't think I even made it to 10:30.

The next thing I knew, my mom was shaking me awake. She pointed my attention to the TV, where I saw myself talking. I was still half-asleep and missed most of the segment.

This was, you will note, a couple of years before the mass-market VCR era, so we had no way of capturing the moment. There is no existing record of this interview, which is too bad.

I would like to see myself doing that somersault in gym class.

These are the non-icky details of my colonoscopy

October 22, 2021: My Cleveland Foundation co-worker Jennifer Cimperman once described me as "earthy," which is a word her mother uses for people who aren't shy about sharing personal details. I am proudly earthy.

I should also mention that the headline is a lie. There are no details of a colonoscopy that aren't icky, but I hoped you would read the first couple of sentences before deciding whether to soldier on or bail before things got messy.

First, let's establish that I am a couple of weeks away from turning 52, which means I was nearly two years late when I underwent my first screening colonoscopy. Actually, if you go by relatively new guidance from the American Cancer Society that such screening should begin at age 45, I was seven years late.

Either way, I should have done this earlier.

I didn't put it off because I was scared of the procedure, though. On the contrary, I am weirdly fascinated by new medical experiences. When I got my first root canal a few years ago, the endodontist had to politely tell me not to ask any more questions so he could actually finish the procedure.

As my wife will confirm, I was really into the specifics when it came to my colonoscopy and the associated prep.

Because of course it's the prep about which everyone has horror stories. And rightly so, given what's involved. The whole goal is to completely clean out all 5 feet of a decidedly unpleasant part of your body: your large intestine.

To do this, you abstain from all solid food the day before your procedure. You're limited to a "clear liquid" diet, which I found out doesn't mean you can only have clear-color liquids. Permissible options include broth, popsicles (no red or purple, though), Jello-O, sports drinks, black coffee or tea, and water. Or at least that was the stuff I had.

That in itself was a bit of a challenge, though I was never as hungry as I thought I would be.

You also have to ingest a certain amount of medicinal liquid designed to really get things moving, if you know what I mean.

It used to be that this liquid was an unpleasant, chalky, nauseating potion. They have apparently advanced the technology, though, because all I had to drink were two 10-ounce bottles of something clear and watery called magnesium citrate.

Now don't get me wrong. You don't want to drink magnesium citrate if you don't have to. It's not especially tasty. But I mixed it with ginger ale and it was fine.

You don't drink this stuff all at once, either. You take in two ounces or so every 10 minutes, and the two bottles are consumed six hours apart. You also swallow four stool softener pills along with the first bottle.

That's all easy enough, but I still managed to screw it up. After you drink magnesium citrate, you're also supposed to drink a large amount of clear liquid, ideally water. At least four full glasses.

I forgot that part. After I finished the first bottle of magnesium citrate and took the pills, I sat back and waited for something to happen.

I waited four hours for something to happen. And nothing did.

OTHER THINGS ON MY MIND

Then I remembered the part about the water. Once I drank that copious amount of H_2O, things did in fact happen.

Oh, they happened.

This is the part where I'll try and skip the icky, but suffice it to say that the sheer physics of the process are horribly illogical. The input/output ratio makes no sense. I think there were traces of Thanksgiving dinner 1981 that passed out of my digestive system.

What comes out way, way, way exceeds the amount of food you've taken in over, say, the past week or so. I still can't understand it.

They tell you you'll be spending a lot of time in the bathroom, and they are correct. I was up until midnight doing what I had to do to get my colon nice and clear.

SPOILER ALERT: As it turns out, I did not do a good enough job with this, and I blame the four-hour delay in drinking water. This oversight would have longer-term consequences, as we will soon see.

Anyway, there were some small aftershocks the next morning, but the bulk of the work had been completed the previous day.

My procedure was scheduled for 1 p.m., and you're supposed to stop eating or drinking four hours prior. Which meant I was finished ingesting anything (even a breath mint) by 9 a.m.

Interestingly, I didn't feel especially tired or weak at that point despite my meager diet of the previous 30 hours. I was actually pretty active that morning. I went and got an e-check on my car, then drove to the BMV to renew my license and registration. I also spent an hour cutting our grass, then broke out my laptop and worked up until almost the moment we left for the endoscopy center.

You have to have someone drive you to the center, by the way. There's a chance you're not going to be in any condition to drive yourself home after the procedure, thanks to the anesthesia, so

Terry had to come with me as I checked in so I could prove I had separate transportation.

I won't go into the boring details of how they get you ready for the actual colonoscopy other than to note the following:

- You have to remove all clothing except your socks and put on a gown that, of course, opens in the back. As I told the nurse, "Oh yeah, that makes sense."

- Speaking of the nurse, she was very pleasant. She and I share a birthday. She stuck some sensors on my shoulder/upper chest and forearm, and also inserted a needle into my hand for the IV. Nothing especially unpleasant.

- Once she left me by myself in the little hospital bed, I had to wait a long time. Or at least it felt like a long time. I thought I would go straight into the procedure room, but it was 30 minutes before they came and got me.

There were a couple of assistants in the procedure room along with the nurse anesthetist and Dr. Khatami, who served as captain of the S.S. Roto Rooter that day.

They were all very pleasant despite the fact they do something like 35 colonoscopies a day (I asked).

We made small talk for a couple of minutes before they instructed me to turn and lay on my left side and bring my knees up toward my chest, which better facilitates the procedure from an anatomical perspective, as you might imagine.

I asked the nurse to fold my pillow for me so I wasn't laying quite so flat, which she did. And that's the last thing I remember, because that was the point when I went night-night.

Or at least I think that was when I went night-night, since it's definitely the last thing I remember. It could be we had more conversation and they had me count to 10 or whatever, but I don't

OTHER THINGS ON MY MIND

recall anything like that happening. If it did, the memory of it was wiped out by Propofol, a wonderful anesthetic often referred to as "milk of amnesia."

I woke up back in the same curtained-off area where they had prepped me. I felt wide awake as the nurse told me my procedure was finished and asked me a couple of questions. I guess I answered them, but then, despite how I felt, I went right back to sleep.

Then I woke up again and she asked if I wanted water, and I said yes. She brought me water, I drank it, and again I fell asleep.

I woke up a third time with the empty water cup laying at my side, and this time I stayed awake. I can't describe how suddenly sleep overtook me those two times after the initial wake-up. I clearly had a good amount of Propofol still in my system.

But then I guess I was fine because I was able to stand up and get myself dressed. I felt a little tired, but nothing too terrible.

After another wait, Dr. Khatami came by to debrief me. The good news: Everything he could see looked fine. No concerns about anything he came across while touring my colon.

The bad news: My clean-out the previous day had not been as thorough as he would have liked, even though I insisted I followed everything to the letter except drinking that darn water. That was apparently my downfall, though, because there was still a lot of "stuff" in there that prevented him from visualizing my entire large intestine.

The result? Instead of being told I was good to go and to come back again for another screening in 10 years, I was instructed to come back "in 3-4 years" so they could take another look. And, adding insult to my injured ego (I thought I had been a model patient), next time I will have to undergo a two-day prep.

Two days.

I should have known this prep had been too easy. So many other people describe the experience as miserable and exhausting.

For me it had just been inconvenient, though certainly very active in terms of restroom trips.

I was given a few photos of the inside of my colon, and in a couple of them you can see areas where waste material covers what should otherwise have been the easily viewed inner lining of my intestine.

Graphic evidence of my failure as a colonoscopy subject.

Oh, the shame.

We'll try it again in 2025.

My failure of the month (and why everyone telling you how great you are at something may not be the best thing)

Every time I put on the headset, I try to be a little better.

January 6, 2023: This isn't a post about my side hustle of sports public address (PA) announcing, but I'm going to use announcing as an example of something I've found to be true both personally and professionally.

By way of context, I do quite a bit of sports PA work in the Cleveland area. When I say "sports PA work," I mean the voice you hear in high school, college or professional gyms, arenas and

5 KIDS, 1 WIFE

stadiums that tells you the starting lineups, who scored, who committed fouls, etc.

In other words, it's the man/woman speaking over the public address system and not, for example, the person doing play-by-play online or over the radio, though I have done some of that.

I have full-time PA announcing gigs at three high schools and regularly sub in at two colleges and a handful of other institutions. I've announced almost every sport you can, from football, soccer, hockey and volleyball to baseball, softball, basketball, track and lacrosse. It's a lot of fun, and a chunk of the money I earn funds an annual scholarship given to a graduating senior from Wickliffe High School.

Altogether, I do more than 100 events each year.

Until a decade ago, I had no idea I possessed any talent for this. But – and I say this with genuine humility, because I am far from the very best person you'll ever hear on the mic – it turns out I'm pretty good at it. Through the accidents of physiology and general brain chemistry, I have a decent PA voice, and my natural rhythm and phrasing are such that I sound somewhat professional.

Again, I'm far from being a true pro, but at the local high school level, I'm likely one of the better PA guys you're going to run across. This is not bragging, it's just a general observation.

So here's the problem.

My philosophy has always been that the announcer should be much like an offensive lineman in football: If he/she does their job well, you hardly know they're there. It can be thrilling, but obviously the athletes on the field or court are why everyone comes. Absolutely *no one* buys a ticket to hear you talk.

Still, people in general tend to be very nice, so I get a lot of compliments on my PA work. I suspect you don't necessarily have to be a great announcer to get people to say good things about you anyway. Often, it's more about the fact that they hear you over

OTHER THINGS ON MY MIND

and over at every game or match, and in their mind your voice becomes associated with happy memories of watching their child, grandchild, niece/nephew, friend, etc. play a sport, no matter how good you actually are.

Anyway, having done this for a number of years, I've received a pretty long list of compliments, all of which are very gratefully received. I personally think I'm probably average to a bit above average at the PA thing and no more, but as I said, the people I come across in the course of this work can be effusive in their praise.

No matter how humble you try to be, hearing how great you are at something can leave you less motivated to get better at it. There's a part of your brain that says you can put it in cruise control because, hey, you're a star, baby!

Sometimes I find myself doing less pregame preparation than I used to because, really, who needs prep when you're already a pro?

This is both silly and dangerous. If I give myself credit for anything when it comes to PA work, it's commitment to detail and preparation. I get confirmation on the pronunciation of every name on the roster, including the seemingly obvious ones like "John Smith." I try and memorize names and uniform numbers so I can quickly deliver the right information. I write down all player substitutions before announcing them because I want them to be 100% accurate. The athletes deserve at least that much from the PA person.

Once you start believing your own hype – even if it's just a string of nice words from well-meaning friends and acquaintances – you stop getting better. And in most cases, you regress.

The parallels to almost anything else in your life, at work or at home, are probably obvious. We should be our own worst critics, though I don't mean that in an unhealthy way. I'm not talking about putting yourself down, but rather continually asking how you can be a better spouse, parent, friend, professional, hobbyist, etc.

It's what business professionals refer to as "continuous improvement."

No matter what compliments you're paid or which honors or awards you receive, don't ever fall into the trap of reading your own press clippings (so to speak).

Want to know the best thing that has happened to me recently? Something that, at first, I didn't think was all that great? It was auditioning for and not getting the PA role for a local lower-level professional sports team. I gave it my best shot, but it wasn't good enough.

I won't lie, at first it stung. It made me go back and reevaluate not just how I did in the actual audition, but in general where I am in terms of my delivery, prep and general approach to announcing. I found some areas where I've been slacking off, so I'm working to correct them such that my overall performance continues to improve, even if slowly and incrementally.

We all love getting a "great job" every once in a while, but in the long run, we probably benefit more from "hey, let's work on this" and even "thanks, but no thanks."

I love the concept of beach vacations. It's the execution that presents problems.

July 10, 2023: As I type this, I'm sitting in the enclosed patio of our rented house in Bethany Beach, Delaware.

Terry is next to me doing some sort of craft that involves creating a picture of Lilo & Stitch from small beads.

Jared is across the table on his laptop writing media notes that are, as he says, of interest only to a very small group of writers and broadcasters covering tonight's Major League Baseball game between his employer, the Tampa Bay Rays, and the Seattle Mariners.

Elissa is to my right crocheting a yarn bikini for the plastic goose that sits in the front window of her house (that statement is 100% true).

Jack is reclining on a nearby chair, playing on his phone.

Light music is coming from Jared's laptop. We are all conversing and laughing.

This, to me, is exactly what vacation should be.

Here's the problem, which I know isn't really a problem at all: The Atlantic Ocean is about 400 feet away. Our nephew Chandler is driving up from his home in Newport News, Virginia, and due to arrive in a half hour or so. Once he gets here, we're all going to change into swimsuits and head to the beach.

That is, after all, why we drove 9 hours from Ohio. This is a beach vacation, and beach vacations by definition involve going to the beach.

I love the idea of going to the beach. And I love the first 10 minutes of being at the beach.

Then it all kind of goes south for me.

I'm not a water guy, but I plan to spend some time in the chilly ocean waters because I would hate to leave here in a few days without having done that.

I'm not a sandcastle builder, but I'll chip in if everyone else is doing it.

The boys and I will toss a ball around, which is fun but after a while makes my 53-year-old rotator cuff cry out for mercy.

We were never a beach vacation family until we first came here to Bethany Beach in 2016 and had a really good time. Seven years later we're back, having coordinated the complicated schedules of eight 20-somethings, a teenager, and two parents.

I wanted to recreate that 2016 vacation, though I realize now that what I wanted to recreate was not so much the beach part of it. It's being together that most appeals to me, whether or not we ever get close to the water.

OTHER THINGS ON MY MIND

There's also this: As I have often noted, I am not a particularly good relaxer. Or at least I don't relax in the same way other people relax.

I almost always need to be doing something. So far on this trip, that has meant playing several games of cribbage, enduring two disastrous losses in Battleship to Jared, washing and putting away the dishes, making our bed, doing some laundry, carding a brisk round of mini-golf, and taking a walk.

Some of those are vacation-type activities while others are not. All of them give me satisfaction because that's just the way I am. Getting stuff done is what I like, whether I'm at home or traveling. I suppose it's how I maintain some semblance of control over my existence.

I admire real beach people. People who can plop down on a chair, slather themselves in sunscreen and read a book for hours. People who don't mind sand in their shoes. People who never tire of frolicking in salt water.

I am not one of them, nor will I ever be. But I admire them.

At the same time, I almost never feel particularly stressed or uptight. I'm perfectly happy the way I am.

You have your way of relaxing, I have mine.

There are sting rays in the ocean, you know. The only foolproof way of avoiding them is not going to the beach at all.

THE GAME SHOWS

While you can argue this entire book is an exercise in self-indulgence, this final section really fits that description. I'm the only one who ever brings up the fact that I was a contestant on both "Who Wants to Be a Millionaire?" (2003) and "The Price Is Right" (2007) because I'm the only one who cares. Still, I mention it often enough that I thought it deserved its own short section.

My 15 minutes (maybe 20) of TV fame were up long ago

That's me in the "Who Wants to Be a Millionaire?" hot seat. My episodes were recorded in October 2002 and aired in late January 2003.

March 14, 2012: Everyone has something interesting they've done in their life. And I do mean everyone. I've never met a person yet who, if you talk to them long enough, won't surprise you with some quirky hobby, experience or brush with fame they've had.

Mine, as my wife will readily tell you, is that I've appeared as a contestant on two game shows: "Who Wants To Be a Millionaire" and "The Price Is Right." I say my wife will tell you because she claims I'm so impressed by this fact about myself that I make a point of bringing it up with any new person I meet.

This isn't true, of course. It's not *any* new person I meet, though I suppose it's accurate to say I mention it to *most* new people I meet.

I readily acknowledge two facts about my game show experience:

1. The whole thing was a lot of dumb luck on my part.

2. The only person who is truly impressed is me. I know this.

Game shows went out of style long ago. When I was growing up, you could turn on the TV almost any time between the hours of, say, 9 a.m. and 5 p.m. and find a game show. And that was when we only had four channels! It was also when our TVs weighed 500 pounds and were steam-powered. And we had to ride our horse and buggy into town if we wanted to watch one of those new-fangled "cable" TV shows.

Anyway, yes, I realize game shows are more mocked than respected these days. This process started 20 years ago and reached its nadir with the retirement of Bob Barker. Bob was the last link to the good old days of game shows, and when he left "The Price Is Right," a piece of the past went out with him.

I actually got to meet Bob when I was on "Price." (That's what we veterans call it: "Price." Well, OK, I'm probably the only who calls it that. Just go with it.) I made the decision to fly out to Los Angeles and attempt to get on the show in 2006, soon after Bob announced that season would be his last as host. No offense to Drew Carey, but if I was ever going to become a contestant, it had to be with Bob.

I also really liked Meredith Vieira, the host of "Who Wants To Be a Millionaire." I was a contestant there during the first season of the syndicated version of the show, which began in 2002 after ABC managed to air the original so many times that Americans got sick of Regis Philbin.

Meredith was very touchy feely. She was always reaching over and patting my shoulder or touching my arm. After the show aired, many people said she was flirting with me. I told them to watch other episodes. Meredith flirted with EVERYBODY. Man or woman, didn't matter to Meredith. Her way of making you feel comfortable in the Hot Seat was to hit on you. I guess it works.

Bob was also very smooth. And tan. Like scary tanned. He was bronzed from head to toe. Given that he lives in Southern California, it was hard to tell how much of it was real and how much was spray-on.

It didn't matter, though, because this was BOB. Right in front of me was Bob Barker. In the flesh. This was the guy I had watched countless times while lying on the couch when I was sick and home from school. The guy who carried that long microphone around and wooed the ladies without even trying. BOB BARKER.

He did have pretty significant crow's feet, of course, but give the guy a break. He was 83 years old at the time. It was clear that, if he wanted, he could still break me in half. Yet he looked you right in the eye when he spoke and treated you like you were the most important contestant in the history of the show. That's something he learned over 35 years of hosting TPIR, I'm sure, but it's also largely an innate talent.

During the commercial breaks, Bob would take questions from the audience, and he was hilarious. These were probably all questions he had been asked a million times before and his answers were likely rehearsed, but it didn't matter. People howled with laughter. Bob was in control of that studio from the moment he walked in.

Speaking of questions, here are the ones people most frequently ask when they find out about the game show thing:

1. **How did I get on?** Like I said, dumb luck. The Millionaire

people held tryouts in Cleveland and I think I just happened to fit their "Goofy White Guy" quota for the day. For Price, my pre-show interview happened to be with a producer with whom I could really relate. He and I clicked. If it had been someone else, I doubt I would have been chosen to "come on down."

2. **How did I do?** I won $32,000 on Millionaire and $2,500 and four electric guitars on Price. One guy in my Millionaire group of contestants won $250,000. It made my $32K look kind of piddly. On Price, I made it all the way to the Showcase Showdown at the end of the show before losing.

3. **What question did I miss on Millionaire?** It was about Mary Cassatt and the kinds of portraits she painted. How come no one ever cares about the 10 questions I got *right*?

4. **Was the big wheel on "Price Is Right" heavy?** Yes, but the last thing you want is to give it a wimpy spin and get booed off the stage. So you try your best to wing it around several times in manly fashion.

5. **Did they take taxes out of your earnings?** The Millionaire people did not, while the Price people took California taxes but not federal taxes. The taxes actually weren't that bad, surprisingly.

6. **What did you do with the money?** Kept my family alive with a roof over their heads. And I think I bought a hockey jersey, too. I'm quite the big spender.

I'm sometimes asked what my next game show will be, and the answer is "none of the above." I think my short-lived TV career is pretty well over. It's nearly impossible to get onto "Jeopardy" and

THE GAME SHOWS

"Wheel of Fortune." And I have no desire to do something like "Survivor" or "Fear Factor." So I'll just keep the DVD recordings of my appearances along with my memories and leave it at that.

And I'll keep my hockey jersey, too. It really is cool.

It's my book and I can talk about the fact I was on two game shows any time I want

September 30, 2015: There are really only two interesting facts about me:

1. I have five children, which in itself isn't really "interesting" since there are a lot of families that have five or more kids.

2. I was a contestant on two nationally televised game shows: "Who Wants to Be a Millionaire" and "The Price Is Right."

The game show thing is territory I've covered before, I realize. So if I'm going to bring it up again, I should have something new to say about it.

Which I do not.

What I DO have to offer is video of my appearances on both shows. Is that enough? Does that justify me taking up a few minutes of your valuable time to discuss it again?

No, it does not.

Yet I'm doing it anyway. Why? Because I still think the whole thing is just so COOL, you know?

I don't write about it because I think it's some great achievement or anything. It was dumb luck I got onto those shows. I write about it because, seriously, how many people do you know who have appeared on two game shows? Not counting me, it has to be zero, right? I'm guessing it is.

To this day, those shows are two of the most remarkable experiences I've had. And it's not going to happen again, given how quickly I am deteriorating mentally. Those two contestant slots are all I'm going to get.

So if you're one of the five or so people I've not yet forced to watch these videos, here they are.

First is my "Who Wants to Be a Millionaire" appearance, which spanned two shows and aired January 30-31, 2003. *(NOTE: In 2022, Sony Entertainment forced me to remove my Millionaire video from YouTube, citing copyright restrictions. So I found a new home for the clip thanks to Vimeo:* https://vimeo.com/736926100?*)*

KEY TAKEAWAY: Meredith Vieira touched me a lot.

I should have won more money, but hey, $32,000 isn't a bad day's work. On to "The Price Is Right." This episode aired on February 16, 2007: https://www.youtube.com/watch?v=AfB_a6cj_jo

And that's it. I'm finished. Really. I will not bring this up again for at LEAST a year. Maybe six months. Four weeks for sure.

OK, I promise I won't mention it tomorrow. Does that work?

This is a quick story about me and Ken Burns

May 21, 2021: When I was on "Who Wants to Be a Millionaire," I correctly answered a question pertaining to documentary filmmaker Ken Burns. It was about the type of documentaries he had produced to that point in 2003, and it was relatively easy for anyone even passingly familiar with his work.

Fast forward about seven years and I'm sitting at the City Club of Cleveland listening to Mr. Burns speak. He was great, as were all of the speakers I used to go and see at the City Club back then.

It's actually one of the biggest things I miss about working in Downtown Cleveland. I became a member of the City Club just for the chance to attend these lunchtime gatherings featuring world-class speakers. It's amazing the array of people I saw there.

When the session ended and everyone in the room headed for the elevators, Mr. Burns was surrounded by people wanting to say hello, shake his hand, ask him questions, etc. He was clearly in a hurry to get out, presumably because he had to be somewhere immediately afterward or was catching a plane.

I patiently followed the little blob of people gathered around him until I could briefly get his attention. I had to walk fast to keep up with him, but when I told him my Millionaire story, he stopped and looked at me.

"Really?" he asked.

"Yes," I said, "true story."

"And you got the question right?"

"I sure did."

"How much was it worth?"

I couldn't remember and told him so, though it was one of the early questions among the 10 I answered correctly.

"Huh," he said. "Being the answer to a question on a game show. That's a new one for me. Thank you for telling me about it."

And he meant it.

Epilogue

Drum major Jack. (Photo by Ron Kotar, used with permission.)

September 9, 2022: We are in the midst of a 10-week period during which Friday nights in our family can only be described as chaotic.

For many years now, our Friday evenings from late August through the end of October have revolved around high school football games and halftime band performances. All of our kids have been members of the Wickliffe Swing Band at one point or another, and my son Jared also kicked for the football team for three years.

At the very least, that has meant hastily consumed dinners,

getting kids to the school on time before a game, and dressing up in our finest Blue Devil gear.

But this year the chaos—again, I can think of no other appropriate word—has ratcheted up exponentially.

Jack, who is enjoying his senior year victory lap, is both co-drum major and band president. These roles encompass a lot, not the least of which is trotting out to midfield at halftime along with his fellow drum major Clare, flinging a baton high into the air, and trying to catch it when it comes back down. All with 90% of people in the stadium watching the two of them. I don't know how nerve-wracking it is for Clare and Jack, but it's terrifying for me.

Terry, who has long volunteered her time to the Swing Band, has taken her involvement this year to a new and presumably unprecedented level ("unprecedented," at least, in Wickliffe band history). She is not only in her second year as Band Booster president and ninth year as chair of the uniform committee, she also recently took on the title of "assistant director." She's now an official Wickliffe City Schools employee and everything. It is risking gross understatement to say she is invested in the success of this ensemble.

My Friday night contributions pale in comparison with Jack's and Terry's, but I'm in my ninth year as the Swing Band announcer as well as my first year as the full-time Wickliffe football PA announcer. The poor people who come to our games cannot escape the reach of my voice without running to their cars.

So fall Fridays are a production. They're also fleeting. If Wickliffe doesn't make the state football playoffs this year, we only have six games to go after tonight. Then, just as suddenly as it began, it will be over.

This time next year, Jack will be in college, Terry will have moved on from her band duties, and while I still plan to announce, it won't feel quite the same.

All of which is why I'm enjoying every second of this season. You would think, with five children (four of whom are out of high school and in their 20s), I would have learned long ago how quickly it all passes and to appreciate it. But until this year, I really hadn't.

For the past decade and a half, we've always had at least one child at the high school, with the promise of more to come. Even last year we knew Jack still had his senior season ahead, so I just jumped from one event to the next without ever stopping to take in the moments and savor them.

Now, with something of a life transition staring us in the face, I find myself pausing on Friday nights and just looking around. I listen to the crowd. I watch Jack march. I observe Terry in her element, doing everything she can to make sure the band is put in the best position to succeed. And I smile at all of it. I take a breath and acknowledge what a special time this is for us.

And how, in no time at all, it will have passed us by.

As recently as a month ago, I dreaded the thought of it ending. But now I don't really mind that much. Just being present in the moment and *knowing* it's a memory in the making changes the whole dynamic. It will end, yes, but that's OK. It's special BECAUSE it's going to end.

At the beginning of every halftime show, I get to announce Jack's name as co-drum major and Terry's name as assistant director (she's only just now getting comfortable with me doing that … not much of a spotlight-seeker, that one). Even counting upcoming band festivals, there are fewer than 10 such opportunities remaining.

With each one, I lean just a little harder into "Jaaaaaaaaaack Tennaaaaaaant!!!" and "assistant director MRS. Terry Tennant!"

What an incredible blessing this has been. And still is. And always will be.

Made in the USA
Las Vegas, NV
08 September 2023

77250296R00108